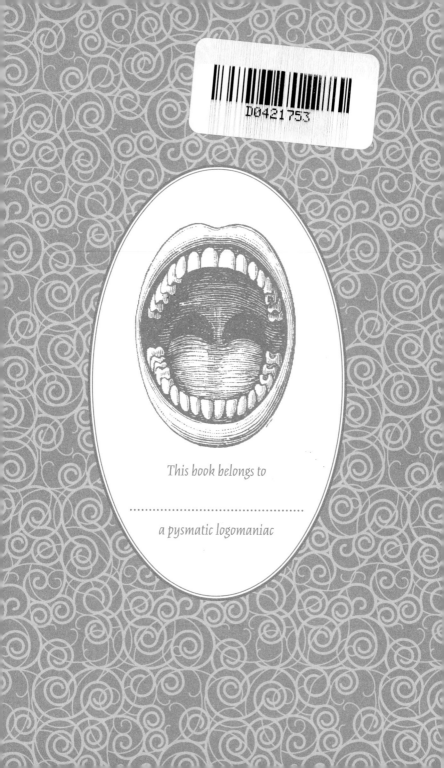

This book belongs to

....

a pysmatic logomaniac

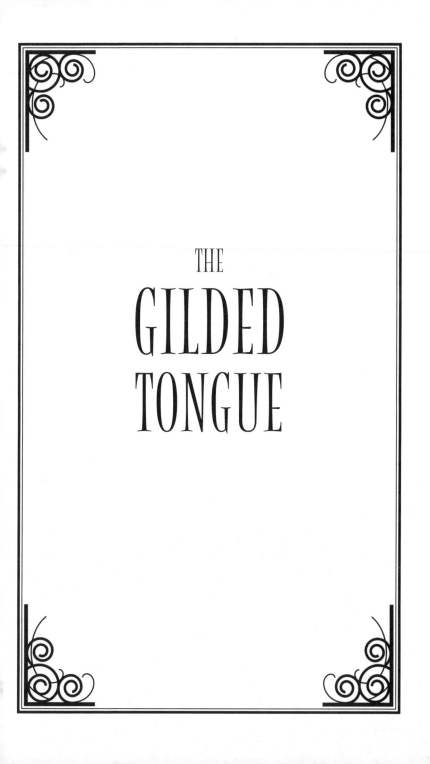

THE
GILDED
TONGUE

THE GILDED TONGUE

Overly Eloquent Words for Everyday Things

ROD L. EVANS, PH.D.

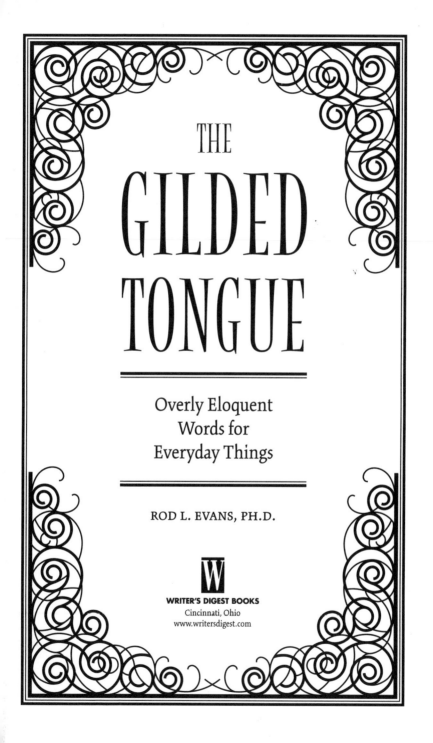

WRITER'S DIGEST BOOKS
Cincinnati, Ohio
www.writersdigest.com

Visit our Web site at www.writersdigest.com for information on more resources for writers.

To receive a free weekly e-mail newsletter delivering tips and updates about writing and about Writer's Digest products, register directly at our Web site at http://newsletters.fwpublications.com.

10   09   08   07   06   5   4   3   2   1

Distributed in Canada by Fraser Direct, 100 Armstrong Avenue, Georgetown, ON, Canada L7G 5S4, Tel: (905) 877-4411. Distributed in the U.K. and Europe by David & Charles, Brunel House, Newton Abbot, Devon, TQ12 4PU, England, Tel: (+44) 1626 323200, Fax: (+44) 1626 323319, E-mail: mail@davidandcharles.co.uk. Distributed in Australia by Capricorn Link, P.O. Box 704, Windsor, NSW 2756 Australia, Tel: (02) 4577-3555.

Library of Congress Cataloging-in-Publication Data
Evans, Rod L.
  The gilded tongue : overly eloquent words for everyday things / Rod L. Evans.-- 1st ed.
      p. cm.
  Includes bibliographical references (p. 214).
  ISBN-13: 978-1-58297-382-1
  ISBN-10: 1-58297-382-2
  1. Vocabulary. 2. English language--Glossaries, vocabularies, etc. I. Title.
  PE1449.E935 2006
  428.1--dc22   2006000539

Edited by Michelle Ehrhard
Designed by Grace Ring
Page layout by Sean Braemer
Production coordinated by Robin Richie

F+W PUBLICATIONS, INC.

ACKNOWLEDGMENTS

My deep thanks go to my literary agent, Sheree Bykofsky, her assistant, Janet Rosen, my editor at Writer's Digest, Michelle Ehrhard, and my good friend and extraordinary administrative assistant, Robin Hudgins. All those people are professionals without whose help this book never would have been published.

INTRODUCTION

We English-speakers are heirs to a rich treasure, a language that has so freely borrowed from other languages as to contain more than one million words. This dictionary contains two interesting subgroups of those words: (i) esoteric (little-known) terms for which there are common single-word synonyms (such as "pugilist," meaning "boxer"), and (ii) esoteric terms for which there are no single-word synonyms but rather synonymous phrases (such as "emacity," meaning "an uncontrollable desire to buy things"). All entries, which appear in at least one unabridged dictionary, describe common phenomena using gilded, highfalutin language.

A NOTE ABOUT THE DEFINITIONS

Sometimes the entries will contain more than one definition. More often, the entries will contain only one definition, either the most popular or the one that is most interesting, at least according to the author.

A NOTE ABOUT PARTS OF SPEECH

Note that most of the entries are nouns (indicated by *n.*) or adjectives (indicated by *adj.*), though some are verbs (indicated by *v.*). Most of the entries belong to only one part of speech, but some can function as, say, nouns or verbs. Because many of the entries carry multiple meanings, it is possible that this dictionary contains the most popular meaning of a term when it occurs as a noun or a verb, but does not contain all the meanings of the term as it functions in all parts of speech. The sentence illustrating the meaning will use the word according to the part of speech ascribed to it in the dictionary.

A NOTE ABOUT WORD ORIGINS

This dictionary contains a brief explanation of the meanings and origins of the roots of words, not a complete etymological analysis. When a word can be traced through several languages, often only the oldest source will be listed, especially when that source is Greek or Latin.

HOW TO USE THIS BOOK

You can use this dictionary in two main ways. First, you can simply pick it up and begin reading anywhere. On any page you'll find some fascinating words that you probably never knew existed. Second, you can find a word by looking at its definition in the reverse dictionary (reversicon) at the end of the book.

USING THE REVERSICON

Although dictionaries usually list the words to be defined in alphabetical order, a reverse dictionary or reversicon lists definitions or descriptions of concepts in alphabetical order and then provides words fitting those definitions. For example, suppose you want to find a word meaning "hatred of marriage," you'll find the appropriate word ("misogamy") in the reverse dictionary of this book under "marriage, hatred of."

Reverse dictionaries are particularly useful when dealing with unusual words for common phenomena, such as "misogamy." Consider another example. Although we are all quite familiar with the metal or plastic tube fixed around each end of a shoelace, we may not know the word "aglet," which describes that item.

This reverse dictionary sometimes contains a few definitions for one term. Accordingly, by the definitions "purgative" and "laxative," you'll see the word "lapactic" because its definitions include ideas associated with both "purgative" and "laxative." Once you look up "lapactic" in the main part of the book, you'll get a clearer sense of its meaning, especially after you see the word used in a sentence.

PRONUNCIATION KEY

(borrowed from Charles H. Elster's *There's A Word for It!: A Grandiloquent Guide to Life*)

VOWEL SOUNDS

A, a—*flat, back, pass, exact*

AH, ah—*spa, father, odd, not*

AHR, ahr—*car, jar, alarm*

AIR, air—*hair, stare, bear*

AY, ay—*hay, wait, came, state*

AW, aw—*raw, all, walk*

E, e—*yes, let, step*

EE, ee—*see, beat, key*

EER, eer—*pier, beer, fear*

I, i—*in, hit, sip*

Y, y and EYE, eye—*by, nice, pie, right, aisle*

> **Note:** *Y* is used in combination with other letters to form a syllable: *SLYT-lee* (slightly). *EYE* is used when this sound by itself forms a syllable: *EYE-land* (island).

OH, oh—*go, sew, coat*

OO, oo—*do, ooze, rule*

OR, or—*for, door, born, war*

OOR, oor—*poor, tour, lure*
OW, ow—*cow, out, tower, doubt*
OY, oy—*oil, loin, boy, ahoy*
UH, uh—*up, dull, some, color; also ago, allow*
UR, ur—*turn, stir, were, learn*
UU, uu—*pull, full, good, took, would*

OBSCURE, UNSTRESSED, LIGHTENED, OR VARIABLE VOWEL SOUNDS

a—*ago, final, woman, librarian*
e—*item, taken, shipment, difference*
i—*edible, policy, charity, nation*
o—*connect, polite, gallop, carrot*
u—*focus, circus, lettuce, raucous*

CONSONANT SOUNDS

B, b—*boy, cab, bubble*
CH, ch—*chip, catcher, peach*
D, d—*dog, add, sudden*
F, f—*fat, effort, staff*
G, g—*get, bigger, bogus, tag*
H, h—*hit, hope, behind*
J, j—*jug, juice, tragic, age*
K, k—*king, cup, take, actor, pack*
L, l—*leg, also, bell*
'l—*ladle, cattle, turtle, apple*
M, m—*my, humble, emblem*
'm—*spasm, prism, chasm, sarcasm*

N, n—*no, knee, end, winner*

'n—*hidden, cotton, open, satin, reason*

NG, ng—*sing, anger, tank*

P, p—*pen, pepper, pop*

R, r—*red, arrive, car*

S, s—*sit, ask, pass*

SH, sh—*she, rush, nation, conscious*

T, t—*top, bitter, list*

TH, th—*thin, thirst, nothing, bath*

TH, th—*there, this, brother, bathe*

V, v—*very, even, live*

W, w—*will, wait, power*

Y, y—*yes, you, layer*

(Y), (y)—indicates that some speakers employ the Y sound of *you* and others do not: N(Y)OO, *new*; D(Y)OO-tee, *duty*; uh-ST(Y)OOT, *astute*

Z, z—*zoo, daze, please*

ZH, zh—*vision, measure, azure*, or French *je*

FOREIGN SOUNDS

KH, kh—German *ach*, Scottish *loch*, Hebrew *l'chaim*: a guttural sound, like that of clearing the throat

(N), (n)—French *vin, bon, blanc, garçon*: a nasalized sound—the N is stopped in the nose

STRESS/ACCENT

• Syllables are separated by a hyphen (-).

• Syllables printed in CAPITAL letters are stressed.

- Syllables printed in small (lowercase) letters are not stressed.

- Words of one syllable are printed in CAPITAL letters.

- Words of more than two syllables that have primary and secondary stress are transcribed in the following manner: The syllable with secondary stress is printed in CAPITALS, and the syllable with primary stress is printed in **BOLDFACED CAPITALS**: ED-i-fi-**KAY**-shin (edification).

THE
DICTIONARY

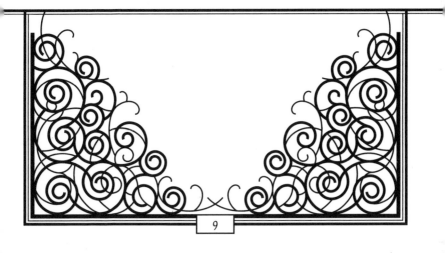

ABDOMINOUS (ab-DAHM-i-nus): *adj.* from Latin *abdomen* (belly, paunch): big-bellied.

The **abdominous** man was not used to exercise.

ABLACTATION (a-blak-TAY-shun): *n.* from past participle of Latin *ablactare* (to wean): the act of weaning.

The infant was crying because he did not adjust well to the **ablactation**.

abdominous

ABSTEMIOUS (ab-STEE-mee-uhs): *adj.* from Latin *abstemius* (abstemious, moderate): sparing or moderate in eating and drinking.

Although Sally was not a teetotaler, she was **abstemious**.

ABULIA (uh-B(Y)OO-lee-uh): *n.* from Greek *a-* (without, not) and *boule* (will): loss or lack of will or motivation, usually expressed by an inability to make decisions or to set goals.

His **abulia** was manifested in his finding it difficult to make even everyday decisions.

ACCUBATION (AK-yoo-**BAY**-shin): *n.* from Latin *accubare* (to recline): the act or practice of reclining on a couch, as practiced by the ancients at meals.

Rush enjoyed lying on the sofa and disliked being disturbed from his **accubation**.

ACEDIA (uh-SEED-ee-uh): *n.* from Greek *akēdia, akēdeia* (without care, anxiety): i. sloth; ii. apathy and inactivity in the practice of virtue; iii. spiritual torpor and apathy.

The strict parent criticized his poorly disciplined son for **acedia**.

ACRITITION (AK-ri-**TISH**-un): *n.* from Greek *a-* (without), Greek *krisis* (crisis), and Latin *coition* (intercourse): sexual intercourse without orgasm.

Because Howard was taught that "real men" always climax during sex, he felt embarrassed by his **acritition**.

ACROAMATIC (**AK**-roh-uh-MAD-ik): *adj.* from Greek *akroamatikos*, from *akroamat-, akroama* (anything heard): told orally to chosen disciples only: esoteric.

Members of Masonic lodges are given **acroamatic** teachings, intended only for the initiated.

AGAMIST (AG-uh-mist): *n.* from Greek *a-* (without, not) and *gamos* (marriage, union): an unmarried person.

The introverted man avoided all romantic relationships and remained a celibate **agamist**.

AGATHIST (AG-uh-thist): *n.* from Greek-derived *agath-* (good): a person who believes all things tend toward ultimate good.

The self-made millionaire was an **agathist**, believing that our setbacks contain the seeds of a greater benefit.

AGATHOKAKOLOGICAL (AG-uh-thoh-KAK-uh-**LAH**-jik-'l): *adj.* from Greek-derived *agath-*, *agathos* (good) and *kako-* (bad, harmful) and English *-logical*: composed of both good and evil.

Dennis the Menace is not purely evil, but, like most of us, is **agathokakological**.

AGLET (AG-lit): *n.* from French *aguillette* (small needle): a metal or plastic tube fixed around each end of a shoelace.

When Jeff's shoelace became caught in the door, the **aglet** was damaged.

AGRAFFE (uh-GRAF): *n.* from French *agrafer* (to hook): the wire cage holding down the cork in a bottle of champagne.

Tom used a screwdriver to remove the **agraffe** from the cork.

AISCHROLATREIA (EYE-skroh-luh-**TRY**-uh): *n.* from Greek *aischros* (shameful, ugly) and *-latreia* (service, worship): worship of filth; cult of the obscene.

agraffe

Although many people regard "shock jock" Howard Stern as profiting from **aischrolatreia**, others regard him simply as a clever entertainer.

ALAE (AY-lee): *n.* from Latin *ala* (a wing, an armpit, a side apartment): fleshy bulbs on each side of the nose.

Everything about W.C. Fields's nose was bulbous, including its **alae**.

ALEATORY (**AY**-lee-uh-TOR-ee): *adj.* from Latin *aleatorius* (of a gambler), from *aleator* (gambler, dice player), from *alea* (a dice game): relating to good or bad luck and especially the risks of bad luck.

aleatory

Because Alex liked predictable things, he found gambling too **aleatory** to be worth his time.

ALLOGRAPH (**AL-**u̲**h**-GRAF): *n.* from Greek *allos* (other) and *-graph* (writing): a signature made by one person for another.

The secretary in the philosophy department signed the **allograph** on behalf of the chair of the department.

ALLOTHEISM (AL-oh-thee-iz'm): *n.* from Greek *allos* (other) and *theos* (god): the worship of foreign or unsanctioned gods.

One of the charges made against Socrates was that he worshiped unsanctioned gods and was guilty of **allotheism**.

ALTEROCENTRIC (AL-tuh-roh-**SEN**-trik): *adj.* from Latin *alter* (other) and *-centric* (English suffix designating center): tending to focus attention and concern on others.

> My **alterocentric** grandmother spends so much time making sure that all others have what they need at dinner that she often neglects herself.

AMADELPHOUS (am-uh-DEL-fuhs): *adj.* from Greek *hama* (together with) and *adelphos* (brotherly), from *adelphos* (brother): gregarious.

> President Clinton has always been known as an **amadelphous** man, feeling at home in crowds and making people feel at home with him.

AMBEER (AM-beer): *n.* probably from *amber*, from its color: tobacco juice.

> When Janine kissed Luke, she tasted the **ambeer** from his chewing tobacco.

AMENTIA (uh-MEN-shee-uh): *n.* from Latin *amentia* (madness, away from mind): mental deficiency, especially resulting from a primary lack of development of intellectual capacity.

> Danny's **amentia** made a college education impossible.

AMOMAXIA (AM-uh-MAX-see-uh): *n.* from the Latin *amo* (to love) and Greek *amaxa* (wagon): lovemaking in a parked car.

Basketball players who engage in **amomaxia** in compact cars should not be surprised if they sprain their backs.

AMPHIGEAN (am-fuh-JEE-uhn): *adj.* from Greek *amphi-* (on both sides, around) and *gaia* (Earth): i. *of a plant or animal*: found in both hemispheres; ii. *of a plant*: having flowers arising from the rootstock.

Although human beings are **amphigean**, penguins are found naturally only in the southern hemisphere.

AMPHIGORY (AM-fi-GOR-ee): *n.* from French *amphigouri* (mishmash): a nonsense verse or composition: a rigmarole with only the appearance of meaning.

Kent enjoyed reading **amphigory** written by Victorian nonsense poets.

AMRITA (uhm-REE-tuh): *n.* in Hinduism, a beverage imparting immortality.

The Greek gods drank nectar, and the Hindu gods drink **amrita**.

AMYLACEOUS (AM-uh-LAY-shuhs): *adj.* from Greek *amylon* (fine meal, starch): of, relating to, or having the characteristics of starch: starchy.

Roland's love of corn, potatoes, rice, and other **amylaceous** foods resulted in his being overweight.

ANALPHABET (an-AL-fuh-bet): *n.* from Greek *analphabētos* (not knowing the alphabet): an illiterate.

Although the young man had no schooling and was an **analphabet**, he was highly intelligent.

ANALYSAND (uh-NAL-uh-sand): *n.* from *analyse* and *-and* (as in multiplicand): one who is receiving psychoanalysis.

People who see psychoan- alysts or psychiatrists will often refer to themselves not as psychiatric patients but as **analysands**.

androcracy

ANDROCRACY (an- DRAHK-ruh-see): *n.* from Greek *andr-* (man, male) and *-cracy* (rule): political and so- cial supremacy of men.

For years many feminists have criticized America as an **androcracy**.

ANHEDONIA (AN-he-**DOH**-nee-uh): *n.* from Greek *an-* (without) and *hēdonē* (pleasure): the inability to experience pleasure or happiness.

It was evident that Todd suffered from **anhedonia** when he wasn't even smiling at his hall of fame induction.

ANORCHOUS (an-ORK-us): *adj.* from Greek *anor- chos*, from Greek *an-* (without) and *orchis* (testicle): with- out testicles.

Near the end of his presidential campaign, the highly refined John Kerry conspicuously went hunting to dilute the image some people had of him as a soft, **anorchous** man.

ANSERINE (AN-suh-ryn): *adj.* from *anserinus*, from *anser* (goose): i. of, relating to, or resembling a goose; ii. silly, stupid.

The teacher chided the class clown for his **anserine** antics.

ANTHROPOPHAGUS (AN-thruh-**PAHF**-uh-GUHS): *n.* from Greek *anthrōphagos* (man-eating): an eater of human flesh; a cannibal.

anthropophagus

The vegetarian would no more dine with meat-eaters than he would dine with an **anthropophagus**.

APOTHEGM (AP-uh-them): *n.* from Greek *apo-phthegma*, from *apo-*, *apo* (far, off, away, separate) and *phthegma* (voice, saying, word): a short, pointed, and instructive saying: a terse aphorism.

I shall never forget my sixth-grade teacher's funny and wise **apothegms**.

ARCADIAN (ahr-KAY-dee-uhn): *n.* from *Arcadia* (from a name of a region of ancient Greece whose inhabitants were viewed as living a simple, pastoral life): a person who lives a simple life of rustic innocence.

A television show once took some Amish **Arcadians** and exposed them to modern life in Los Angeles.

ARRANT (AR/AIR-uhnt): *adj.* from alternation of *errant*: out-and-out, thoroughgoing, extreme (often used derogatorily).

Becky regarded her ex-boyfriend as an **arrant** liar after she found out about his many affairs.

ASPERGE (uh-SPUHRJ): *v.* from Middle French *asperger*, from Latin *aspergere* (to sprinkle): to sprinkle, especially with holy water.

During the performance of *Peter Pan*, Tinkerbell **asperged** everyone—even members of the audience—with glittering fairy dust.

AUBADE (oh-BAHD): *n.* from French, from Old Provençal *auba*, *alba* (dawn): i. a song or poem greeting the dawn; ii. a morning love song; iii. morning music.

The canary warbled an **aubade**, greeting the morning sun.

AUTARKY (AW-tahr-kee): *n.* from modification of German *autarkie*, from Greek *autarkeia* (personal self-sufficiency), from *autarkēs* (self-sufficient): self-sufficiency, independence, especially national economic self-sufficiency, under which countries don't require imports to survive.

The politician was not calling for pure **autarky**, just for a large reduction in oil imports.

BAGNIO (BAN-yoh): *n.* from Italian *bagno*, from Latin *balneum*, from Greek *balaneion*; akin to Greek *balaneus* (bather): a house of prostitution; brothel.

> The angry conservative accused President Clinton of debasing the White House by turning it into a **bagnio**.

BANAUSIC (buh-NAW-sik): *adj.* from Greek *banausikos* (of artisans), from *banausos* (artisan): i. governed by or suggestive of practical or utilitarian purposes; ii. moneymaking, breadwinning: vocational.

> Simon was a practical man whose mind was always directed toward **banausic** and immediately useful pursuits.

BARATHRUM (BAR-uh-thruhm): *n.* from Greek *barathron* (a pit, gulf): i. a deep pit in Athens into which criminals condemned to death were thrown; ii. a bottomless pit or abyss (Hell); iii. an insatiable glutton.

> Even though Carl grew up a coal miner's son, he couldn't help thinking of the mine as anything but a **barathrum**.

BARM (bahrm): *n.* from Old English *beorma*; akin to Middle Low German *barm* (yeast): beer foam.

> Bubba loved to lick the **barm** on top of his beer.

barm

BATHYCOLPIAN (BATH-i- **KAHL**-pee-in): *adj.* from Greek *bathys* (deep) and *kolpos* (bosom): having large bosoms with deep cleavage.

Dolly Parton is known for her **bathycolpian** body.

BATRACHOPHAGOUS (BA-truh-**KAHF**-uh-gus): *adj.* from Greek *batrachos* (frog) and *phagein* (to eat): frog-eating.

Although we normally would not describe people as **batrachophagous**, many people eat and enjoy frog legs.

BELGARD (bel-GAHRD): *n.* from Italian *bel guardo* (lovely look): a kind or loving look.

Nancy gave Ron a **belgard** as she reached for his hand.

BÊTISE (bay-TEEZ): *n.* from French *bête* (beast, fool, foolish), from Old French *beste* (beast): foolish act or remark.

When Dan said that he wanted to learn Latin to be able to talk with Latin Americans, we weren't sure whether his **bêtise** was sincere.

BIBLIOPHAGE (BIB-lee-oh-**FAYJ**): *n.* from Greek-derived *biblio-* (book, paper, scroll) and *-phage*, from *phagein* (to eat): bookworm (literally or figuratively).

bibliophage

On the TV show *Batman* Roddy McDowall played a **bibliophage** appropriately called The Bookworm.

BIBLIOPOLE (**BIB**-lee-uh-POHL): *n.* from Latin *bibliopola* (bookseller), from Greek *bibliopōlē*, from *biblio-*, *biblos* (paper, book scroll) and *poleo* (to sell, barter): a dealer in books, especially used or rare ones.

> Tommy Warren, a **bibliopole** in Norfolk, Virginia, has one of the largest collections of used books on the East Coast.

BIBULOUS (BIB-yuh-lus): *adj.* from Latin *bibulus*, from *bibere* (to drink): fond of drinking, especially excessively.

> Although the entertainer Dean Martin pretended to be **bibulous**, he was moderate in his drinking habits.

BLATHERSKITE (**BLATH**-uhr-SKYT): *n.* from *blather* (to talk nonsensically) and English dialectal *skite* (a contemptible person): i. a babbling, foolish person; ii. blather.

> Becky was a **blatherskite** who pretended to have a deep knowledge of several disciplines, even though she was often caught making inaccurate statements.

BOEOTIAN (bee-OH-shin): *adj.* from *Boeotia*, a district in ancient Greece thought backward by Athenians: marked by stupidity and philistinism; crudely obtuse.

> Many fashionable people on both coasts of America regard conservatives in the South and the Midwest as hopelessly **Boeotian**.

BORBORYGMUS (BOR-bor-**RIG**-mu̲s): *n.* from Greek *borborygmos*, from *borboryzein* (to rumble): a rumbling sound made by the movement of gas in the intestine.

> Ann chose carefully from the menu because she didn't want to be embarrassed by any unpleasant **borborygmus** on the first date.

BOSKY (BAHS-kee): *adj.* from English dialect *bosk* (bush), from Middle English and English -*y*: i. having an abundance of bushes, shrubs, or trees; ii. wooded.

> Jasmine was temporarily lost after having entered a **bosky** section of the park.

BRABBLE (BRAB-uhl): *v.* from Middle Dutch *brabbelen* (to quarrel, stammer, jabber, of imitative origin): to talk noisily or captiously.

> The boisterous woman at the beauty parlor would **brabble** about anything that didn't perfectly suit her.

BRIO (BREE-oh): *n.* from Italian, of Celtic origin; akin to Old Irish *brīg* (strength, virtue), Welsh *bri* (repute), Cornish *bry* (worth), Middle Breton *bri* (regard): vivacity, spirit.

> The singer sang with such **brio** that the audience felt exhilarated.

BROBDINGNAGIAN (BRAWB-ding-**NAG**-ee-uhn): *adj.* from *Brobdingnag*, a country in Jonathan Swift's *Gulliver's Travels*, where everything is enormous: immense, enormous.

The comedian Jimmy Durante was famous for his **Brobdingnagian** nose.

BRUMMAGEM (BRUHM-uh-juhm): *adj.* from *Brummagem*, alteration of *Birmingham*, England, from the fact that in the seventeenth century notorious counterfeit coins were produced in Birmingham, and that in the nineteenth century various cheap and flimsy articles were manufactured there: cheap and showy; phony, sham.

The pimp loved his **brummagem** jewelry.

BRUXOMANIA (BRUHKS-uh-**MAY**-nee-uh): *n.* from New Latin, from Greek *brychein* (to gnash the teeth) and *-mania* (frenzy, madness): the act or practice of grinding one's teeth.

When her nemesis would enter the room, Nora's blood pressure would rise, and she would suffer from **bruxomania**.

BUTYRACEOUS (BYOO-ti-**RAY**-shus): *adj.* from Latin *butyrum* (butter) and English *-aceous* (pertaining to, having the nature of): having the qualities of butter; resembling butter.

The old yellow can of paint we found in the basement was so **butyraceous** that we decided against using it on the walls.

butyraceous

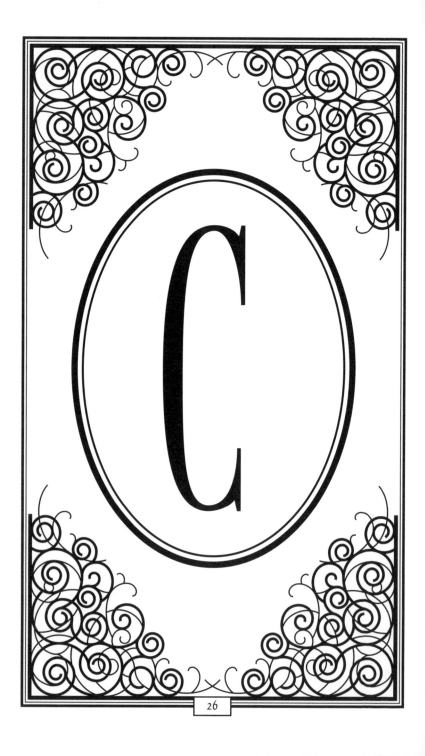

CACHINNATE (KAK-i-nayt): *v.* from Greek *kachazein* (to laugh loudly), from Sanskrit *kakhati* (he laughs): to laugh, usually loudly or convulsively.

> Some funny movies make people **cachinnate** until they cry.

CACOËTHES (KAK-oh-**EE**-theez): *n.* from Greek *kakoēthes* (wickedness), from neuter of *kakoēthēs* [malignant, from *kak-*, *cac-* and *-ēthēs*, from *ēthos* (custom)]: a habitual and uncontrollable desire; mania.

> Although some men viewed President Clinton's serial affairs as evidence of enviable virility, others saw his extramarital sexual appetite as a **cacoëthes**.

CAGAMOSIS (KAG-uh-**MOH**-sis): *n.* from Greek *kakos* (bad) and *gamos* (marriage): marital unhappiness.

cagamosis

> A **cagamosis** can be good news to a divorce attorney.

CAITIFF (KAY-tif): *n.* from Middle English *caitif*, from Norman French (captive, miserable, vile), from Latin *captivus* (captive): a base, wicked, and cowardly person.

> Instead of fighting against American soldiers, Saddam Hussein hid in holes like a **caitiff**.

CALLIPYGIAN (KAL-i-**PIJ**-ee-in): *adj.* from Greek *kallipygos*, from *kalli-* (beautiful) and *pyge* (buttocks): having shapely buttocks.

A **callipygian** woman with a decent singing voice and a good agent can often make more money than a woman with an unattractive body and an excellent singing voice.

CANESCENT (kuh-NES-uhnt): *adj.* from Latin *canescere*, from *canere* (to be gray, be white), from *canus* (white, hoary): growing white, whitish, or hoary.

The full moon was **canescent**.

CAPTIOUS (KAP-shuhs): *adj.* from Latin *captiosus*, from *captio* (act of taking, deception, fallacious argument): i. calculated to confuse, entrap, or entangle in argument; ii. marked by an inclination to stress faults and raise often trivial objections.

Her criticisms of the president were viewed as **captious** and partisan.

CATHOLICON (kuh-**THOL**-i-KAHN): *n.* from Middle English, from Old French, from Medieval Latin, from Greek *katholikon* (generic description), from neuter of *katholikos* (universal): a universal remedy; a panacea.

catholicon

Late-night TV often contains advertisements of supposed **catholicons**.

CHREMATISTIC (KREE-muh-**TIS**-tik): *adj.* from Greek *chrēmatistikos* (of business or moneymaking), from *chrēmatistēs* (businessman): of, relating to, or occupied in gaining wealth.

Donald Trump has interests going beyond the **chrematistic**; he is also interested in his hair.

CHRESTOMATHIC (KRES-tuh-**MATH**-ik): *adj.* from Greek *chrēstomatheia* (learning that is good or useful): belonging to, or devoted to, useful knowledge or learning.

The motivational speaker Brian Tracy likes to remind people that, if they want to become more marketable, they must regularly devote time to **chrestomathic** pursuits.

CIRCUMJACENT (SUR-kuhm-**JAY**-sent): *adj.* from Latin *circumjacens*, present participle of *circumjacere*, from *circum-* (around, about) and *jacere* (to lie): surrounding.

The genius referred to his co-workers as his "**circumjacent** idiots."

CLAUDICATION (CLAW-di-**KAY**-shin): *n.* from *claudicare* (to limp): lameness, limping.

When we saw Ricky walk after being tackled, we immediately noticed his **claudication**.

CLEPTOBIOSIS (KLEP-toh-by-**OH**-sis): *n.* from Greek-derived *klepto-* (theft), from *kleptein* (to steal) and *-biosis* (mode of life): the act of plundering food, as when members of one species steal food from another species.

Some species of ants will engage in **cleptobiosis** for food.

CLERISY (KLER-uh-see): *n.* from German *klerisei* (clergy, often used contemptuously), from Medieval Latin *clericia*, from Late Latin *clericus* (priest): the well-educated or learned class; the literati; the intelligentsia.

Many people believe that ordinary people are often more aware of reality than the **clerisy**.

COACTION (koh-AK-shin): *n.* from Latin *coactio* (a collecting, collection): compulsion.

Both Jefferson and Madison believed that the state should avoid **coaction** in matters of religious conscience.

COCKALORUM (KAHK-uh-lor-uhm): *n.* probably from a modification of obsolete Flemish *kockeloeren* (to crow, of imitative origin): a small, boastful, or self-important man; a little man who thinks he's big.

The deeds of a **cockalorum** never equal his words.

COGNOMEN (kahg-NOH-muhn): *n.* from Latin *co-* (with, together) and *nomen* (name): a family name; a surname.

When the police officer asked for Brad's last name, Brad replied that he never reveals his **cognomen** to strangers.

COLLOCATE (**KAHL**-uh-KAYT): *v.* from Latin *collocare*, from *com-*, *cum* (together, with) and *locare* (to place): i. to set or place together or in proper order; ii. to arrange side by side.

Bessie removed the books from the table and neatly **collocated** them on the bookshelf.

COLPORTEUR (KAHL-por-tur): *n.* from French *colporteur*, alteration influenced by *porter á col* (to carry on one's back, literally, neck) of Middle French *comporteur* (from *comporter*, to hawk, peddle, carry): a peddler of books, especially the Bible and other religious books.

Because of the prevalence of bookstores and the availability of inexpensive books on the Internet, people nowadays rarely encounter **colporteurs**.

COMESTIBLE (kuh-MES-tuh-buhl): *adj.* from Middle French, from Medieval Latin *comestibilis*, from Latin *comestus*, past participle of *comedere* (to eat up): edible.

Although some people with mineral deficiencies will sometimes consume dirt, it is normally not considered **comestible** by human beings.

COMMENSALITY (kuh-men-SAHL-i-tee): *n.* from Latin *cum* (with, together) and *mensa* (table): the practice of eating together.

The sociologist asserted that families that practice **commensality** have fewer problems than families who don't.

CONCLAMANT (KAHN-klay-muhnt): *adj.* from *conclamans*, present participle of *conclamare* (to shout or bewail together): crying out together.

The two sons expressed their dissatisfaction with their mother's dinner in **conclamant** voices.

CONGERIES (**KAHN**-juh-REEZ): *n.* from Latin *congerere* (to bring together): a collection or aggregation, as of ideas, forces, or individuals.

Society has been called a **congeries** of impermanent groupings.

COPROLOGY (kuh-PRAHL-uh-jee): *n.* from Greek *kopros* (dung) and *-logy* (knowledge, science, study of): study of pornography.

The prudish man stated that any study of D.H. Lawrence's *Lady Chatterley's Lover* automatically involves **coprology**.

COPROPHAGOUS (kuh-PRAHF-uh-gus): *adj.* from Greek *kopros* (dung) and *phagein* (to eat): dung-eating.

Certain insects are **coprophagous**, though human beings find excrement unappetizing.

COSSET (KAHS-it): *v.* possibly from Anglo-Norman *coscet* (pet lamb), from Middle English *cotsete* (cottage-dweller): to pamper or treat as a pet.

When parents **cosset** their children, they can make it more difficult for them to develop self-reliance as they become adults.

COSTIVE (KAHS-tiv): *adj.* from Latin *constipare* (to crowd together): i. constipated or causing constipation; ii. slow or stiff in action or expression: sluggish.

costive

Because of red tape, bureaucracies are almost inevitably **costive**, rarely accomplishing any major task swiftly.

COULISSE (koo-LEES): *n.* from French (groove, door, window, or partition that slides in a groove), from Old French *couleice* (literally, sliding door): i. a side of the stage in a theater; ii. a place behind the scenes, such as a lobby or corridor.

The robbery took place in some **coulisse**, away from the crowd of people .

CREPITATION (KREP-i-**TAY**-shin): *n.* from Latin *crepitare* (to crackle): a crackling sound or crackling.

The campfire produced **crepitation** when the fresh log was consumed.

CRUCIFEROUS (kroo-SIF-ur-us): *adj.* from Latin *cruc-*, *crux* (cross) and *-fer*, *fero* (carry, bear): bearing or carrying a cross, as in an ecclesiastical procession.

Jane felt her **cruciferous** workload after the new merger was unacknowledged by her superiors.

CRUCIVERBALIST (**KROO**-suh-VUR-buhl-list): *n.* from Latin *cruci-*, *crux* (cross) and *verbum* (word): a person adept at creating or solving crossword puzzles.

Some **cruciverbalists** are so skillful that they can solve *The New York Times* crossword puzzle in less than fifteen minutes.

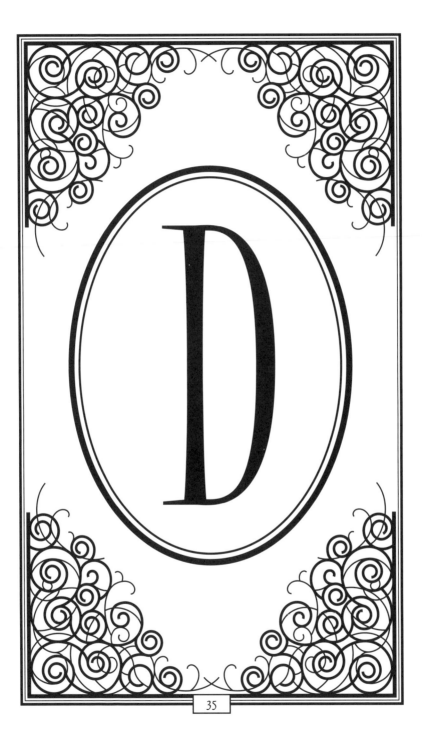

DAEDALIAN (di-DAY-lee-in): *adj.* from *Daedalus* (mythical craftsman and inventor of ancient Greece who constructed the Labyrinth to contain the Minotaur and who invented wings with which he escaped imprisonment): relating to, or suggesting the cleverness of, Daedalus.

> The mechanic pointed out the **Daedalian** devices on the car for temporarily shutting down the air conditioner to give the car additional power during acceleration.

DANDLE (DAN-duhl): *v.* origin unknown: i. to move (a small child) up and down on the knees or in the arms playfully; ii. to pamper or pet.

dandle

> The infant loved to be **dandled** on his mother's knees.

DEFALCATION (DEE-fal-**KAY**-shin): *n.* from Medieval Latin *defalcare* (to mow, deduct): misappropriation or embezzlement of funds.

> The executive was charged with **defalcation** when he bought a swimming pool with money that was supposed to be used for advertising.

DEGUST (di/dee-GUHST): *v.* from Latin *degustare*, from *de-* (from, off, apart, away, down) and *gustare* (to taste): to taste with relish; savor.

Troy loved to **degust** almost every item on the buffet.

DEIPAROUS (dee-IP-uh-r<u>us</u>): *adj.* from Latin *deus* (god) and *parere* (to bring forth): giving birth to a god—said of the Virgin Mary.

> Because of Michael Jordan's almost divine prowess, his mother might be considered **deiparous**.

DEIPNOSOPHY (dyp-NAHS-uh-fee): *n.* from *deipnon* (meal), probably of non-Indo-European origin and Greek *sophistēs* (wise man, sophist): skillful dinner conversation.

> Oscar Wilde was so skilled at **deipnosophy** that he received many free dinners from people who loved to hear him talk.

DERMAGRAPHISM (DUR-muh-**GRAF**-iz'm): *n.* from Greek *derma* (skin, hide) and English *-graphism* (writing): the practice of leaving marks on the skin of a romantic partner by biting, scratching, or sucking: the practice of producing hickeys.

> The physician immediately identified the marks on Peter's neck as evidence of **dermagraphism**.

DESIPIENCE (dee-SIP-ee-ents): *n.* from Latin *desipientia* (folly): relaxed dallying in enjoyment of foolish trifles.

> The boss was all business and had no patience for Melvin's **desipience** in the workplace.

DIASTEMA (DY-uh-**STEE**-muh): *n.* from New Latin, from Late Latin, from Greek *diastēma* (space between, interval): the space or gap between teeth in a jaw.

Sometimes dental floss can get caught in a **diastema**.

DILACERATE (di-LAS-ur-ayt): *v.* from Latin *dilaceratus*, past participle of *dilacerare*, from *di-*, from *dis-* (apart) and *lacerare* (to tear): to tear apart or in pieces.

When the traffic cop learned about the speeder's hard luck, he began to **dilacerate** the ticket.

DIPSOMANIA (DIP-suh-**MAY**-nee-uh): *n.* from New Latin, from *dipso-*, from Greek *dipsa* (thirst) and *mania* (frenzy, madness): an uncontrollable and often periodic craving for alcohol; alcoholism.

Although many excellent writers have suffered from **dipsomania**, excessive drinking rarely, if ever, aids the creative process.

DOBBIN (DAHB-uhn): *n.* from *Dobbin*, alteration of *Robin*, nickname for Robert: a horse, especially a working farm horse.

Fred hitched the plow to the **dobbin**.

DOLORIFUGE (duh-LOR-i-fyooj): *n.* from Latin *dolor* (ache, pain, grief) and *fugere* (to flee): something that banishes or mitigates pain or grief.

When feeling down, Timmy would often rent a funny movie as a **dolorifuge**.

DOMPT (DAHM(P)T): *v.* from French *dompter* (to tame), from Latin *domitare*, from *domare* (to tame): to hold (as a lion) at bay.

The lion tamer was mauled because of his inability to **dompt** the lion.

DORSODYNIA (DOR-soh-DIN-ee-uh): *n.* from Latin *dorsum* (back) and *-dynia*, *dye* (pain, misery): back pain.

Jerry's **dorsodynia** was so bad that he had to sleep on the floor to avoid constant pain.

dorsodynia

DRATCHELL (DRACH´l): *n.* origin uncertain, though possibly from Scottish *drotch* (to hang negligently): i. a lazy and loose woman; ii. slut.

The young Mormon was shocked when he was accosted by a drunken **dratchell** looking for sex.

DUENDE (doo-**EN**-DAY): *n.* from Spanish dialectal (charm), from Spanish (ghost): the ability to attract others through personal magnetism and charm.

Bob's ability to get along with others and his **duende** enabled him to outsell his competitors.

DUNCICAL (DUHN-si-kuhl): *adj.* from *dunce*, from theologian John *Duns Scotus*, whose writings and philosophy were ridiculed in the sixteenth century: stupid.

Young people who participate in drinking contests can suffer gravely for their **duncical** behavior.

DUNDREARIES (DUHN-DREER-eez): *n.* from Lord *Dundreary*, character in the play *Our American Cousin* by Tom Taylor: long flowing side whiskers.

Men commonly wore **dundrearies** not only in nineteenth-century America but also during the 1960s.

dundrearies

DYSCHEZIA (dis-KEE-zee-uh): *n.* from Greek-derived *dys-* (difficult) and *chezo* (to defecate): difficulty and pain in defecating.

Reggie's **dyschezia** was most likely caused by a diet high in cheese and low in fiber.

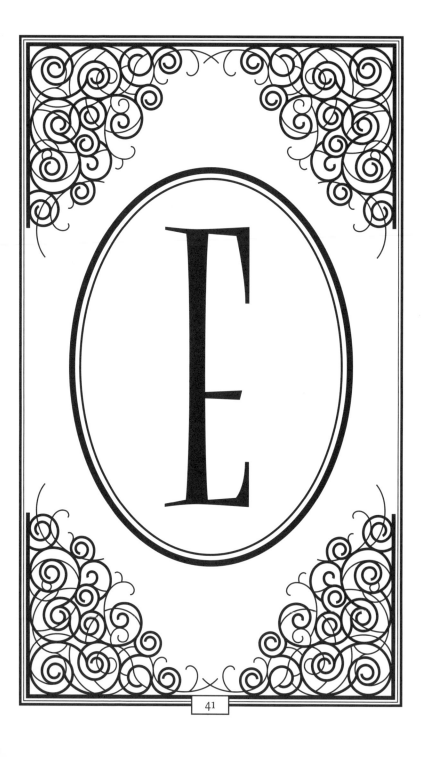

EDACITY (ee-DAS-i-tee): *n.* from Latin *edacitas,* from *edac-, edax,* from *edere* (to eat): the quality or state of being voracious; extraordinarily hungry.

> The tremendous wrestler Andre the Giant was known for his **edacity**.

ELEUTHEROPHILIST (i-LOO-thur-**AHF**-uh-list): *n.* from Greek *eleutheria* (freedom) and *philein* (to love): someone who advocates free love.

> The **eleutherophilist** was criticized for advocating sex without commitment.

EMACITY (ee-MAS-i-tee): *n.* from Latin *emacitas* (fond of buying), from *emere* (to buy): an uncontrollable desire to buy things.

> Because of Amy's **emacity**, she had accumulated more than ten thousand dollars of consumer debt.

EMBRASURE (em-BRAY-zhur): *n.* from French, from obsolete *embraser* (to widen an opening): the sloped valley or gap between adjacent teeth (as in the human mouth).

> David Letterman's smile reveals a highly noticeable **embrasure** between his two front teeth.

EMINENTO (EM-uh-**NEN**-toh): *n.* from a modification of the Italian *eminente*: an eminent person.

> Bill Gates has become an **eminento** in the world of computers because of the success of his company Microsoft.

EMPLEOMANIA (EM-plee-oh-**MAY**-nee-uh): *n.* from Spanish *empleomania*, from *empleo* (employment, use, public office), from *emplear* (to employ, use), from Old Spanish, from Old French *empleoir*, *emploiier*, and Greek *-mania* (madness, frenzy): a mania for holding public office.

> William Jennings Bryan must have been stricken by **empleomania** to have run unsuccessfully three times for the American presidency.

ENOLOGY (ee-NAHL-uh-jee): *n.* from Greek *oinos*: the science of wine or winemaking, viticulture.

enology

> Because Selma's father owned a winery, she knew a great deal about **enology**.

EPHECTIC (e-FEK-tik): *adj.* from Greek *ephektikos* (to hold back): habitually suspending judgment.

> Misty was too **ephectic** ever to commit herself to any unwavering conviction.

ESCRITOIRE (**ES**-kruh-TWAHR): *n.* from obsolete French *escritoire* (writing desk), from Medieval Latin *scriptorium*: a writing table or desk.

> Years ago **escritoires** were as common as computer stations are today.

ESCUTCHEON (e-SKUHCH-in): *n.* from Middle English *escochon*, from Middle French *escuchon*, from (assumed) Vulgar Latin *scution-*, from Latin *scutum* (shield): a decorative metal plate around a keyhole, door lock, doorknob, or the handle of a drawer.

escutcheon

The **escutcheon** around the keyhole was highly ornate.

ESTIVAL (ES-tuh-vuhl): *adj.* from Middle English *estival*, from Middle French, from Latin *aestivalis*, from *aestivus* (of summer), from *aestas* (summer): of, relating to, or appearing in the summer.

Teachers often enjoy their **estival** vacations as much as students do.

EUNOMY (YOO-nuh-mee): *n.* from Greek *eunomia*, from *eunomos* (having good laws): civil order under good laws.

If the human race is to flourish, **eunomy** must replace violence.

EUPEPTIC (yoo-PEP-tik): *adj.* from Greek *eupeptos*, from *eu-* (good, well), and *peptein* (to digest): i. relating to or having good digestion; ii. conducive to good digestion; iii. cheerful, happy.

Justin was a naturally **eupeptic** man who would rarely allow anything to depress him.

EXIGUOUS (ig-ZIG-yoo-uhs): *adj.* from Latin *exiguus*, from *exigere* (to measure out, drive out, demand): extremely scanty.

The young man eked out a living on an **exiguous** income.

EXIMIOUS (ek-SIM-ee-u̱s): *adj.* from Latin *eximius*, from *eximere* (to take out, remove, free): select, choice, excellent.

The *Oxford English Dictionary* is esteemed as an **eximious** reference.

EXOGAMY (eks-AHG-uh-mee): *n.* from Greek-derived *ex-* (out of, without) and *-gamy* (marriage, union): marriage outside a specific group, especially as required by law or custom: outbreeding.

Although interracial marriages are more widely accepted in America than ever before, that form of **exogamy** is still not universally accepted.

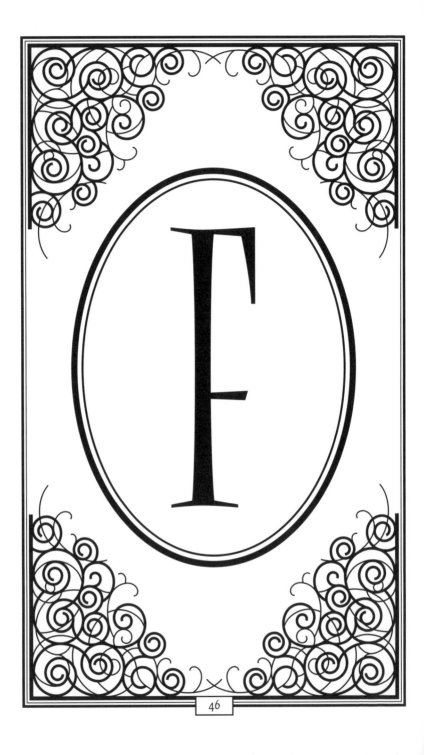

FACUNDITY (fa-KUH-duh-tee/dee): *n.* from Latin *facunditas* (talkativeness): eloquence.

Although the scholar was rightly praised for his **facundity**, he was rarely quotable.

FAINÉANT (FAY-nee-int): *n.* from French *fainéant*, from Middle French *fait-nient* (literally, [he] does nothing): an irresponsible or weak idler.

Before Ted became a millionaire from his laundry business, many of his acquaintances regarded him as an amiable **fainéant** who would never have a strong sense of purpose.

FAMULUS (FAM-yuh-lus): *n.* from Latin *famulus* (servant): a private secretary or attendant, especially of a scholar or magician.

famulus

The scholar would often call on his **famulus** to type for him.

FANTODS (FAN-tahds): *n.* origin unknown: i. a state of nervous irritability; ii. an outburst of emotion; a fit.

We could not be calm when Nelly suffered the **fantods**.

FARCI (fahr-SEE): *adj.* from French past participle of *farcir* (to stuff, from Old French): stuffed, especially with finely ground meat.

We especially enjoyed the mushrooms **farci**.

FARD (FAHRD): *v.* from Middle English *farden*, from Middle French *farder*, of Germanic origin; akin to Old High German *faro* (colored): to paint the face with cosmetics.

fard

We thought that Tammy's thickly **farded** cheeks made her look tawdry.

FARRAGO (fuh-RAH-goh): *n.* from Latin *farrago* (mixed fodder for cattle, mash, mixture): i. mixture, medley; ii. a confused, disordered, or irrational assemblage (as of words or ideas).

The angry student called the teacher's historical lecture a **farrago** of half-truths and misrepresentations.

FATIDIC (fay/fuh-TID-ik): *adj.* from Latin *fatidicus* (prophet): of or belonging to prophecy: prophetic.

The scientist questioned the accuracy of Nostradamus's **fatidic** passages.

FAUNOIPHILIA (FAW-noy-**FIL**-ee-uh): *n.* from Latin *Fauna* (Roman god of nature and fertility), Greek *koinonia* (copulation), and Greek *philia* (love, fondness): an abnormal desire to watch animals copulate.

Bubba's **faunoiphilia** led him to follow cats in heat.

FELICITATE (fi-**LIS**-i-TAYT): *v.* from Latin *felicitare* (to make happy), from *felicitas* (felicity): to congratulate.

We wanted to **felicitate** the new mayor on his victory.

FENESTRATED (fen-uh-STRAYD-id): *adj.* from Latin *fenestrare* (to provide with openings or windows), from *fenestra* (opening, window): provided with or characterized by windows.

Although most students enjoy being in **fenestrated** rooms, a view of the outdoors can be a distraction to learning.

FERACIOUS (fuh-RAY-shuhs): *adj.* from Latin *ferre* (to bear): producing abundantly; prolific, fruitful.

The farmer's **feracious** orchard gave him a good living.

FERIATION (FEER-ee-**AY**-shin): *n.* from Medieval Latin *feriatio*, from Latin *feriatus*, past participle of *feriari* (to rest from work, keep holiday): the practice of observing a holiday; the act of taking time off work.

Because of Belinda's hectic work schedule, she looked forward to periods of **feriation**.

FESCENNINE (FES-uh-nin, FES-uh-nyn): *adj.* from Latin *fescenninus*, probably from *Fescenninus*, from *Fescennium*, ancient town in Etruria, Italy, famous for bawdy songs and verses: obscene, lewd.

There was a warning label on the CD to caution parents about the **fescennine** lyrics.

FETOR (FEE-tuhr): *n.* from Latin *fetor*, from *fetere* (to stink): an offensive odor.

The rebellious adolescent took perverse pride in the **fetor** of his farts.

FIDEISM (FY-de-iz'm): *n.* from Latin *fides* (faith): any doctrine according to which all or some knowledge depends on faith or revelation rather than reason.

When it came to financial investments, Seymour made decisions based on appeals to evidence and rejected **fideism**.

FILIPENDULOUS (fil-i-PEN-dyoo-luhs): *adj.* from Latin *filum* (thread) and *pendulus* (hanging): i. suspended by a thread; ii. as if suspended by a thread.

The fluctuations in the stock market caused Sidney to regard his investments as **filipendulous**.

FLEBILE (FLEB-uhl): *adj.* from Latin *flebilis* (lamentable, wretched): tearful, doleful.

Scott appeared to be humiliated during his **flebile** apology.

FLETCHERIZE (FLECH-ur-**YZ**): *v.* from Horace *Fletcher*, health advocate, who suggested chewing food at least thirty times before swallowing: to reduce food to tiny particles, especially by chewing at least thirty times.

If people want to avoid indigestion, they'd do well to **fletcherize** their food before swallowing it.

FLEXUOUS (FLEK-shoo-uhs): *adj.* from Latin *flexuosus*, from *flexus* (a bending, a turning): bending or winding; sinuous.

We had to slow the car down because we encountered a **flexuous** stretch of road.

FOOTPAD (FUUT-pad): *n.* from English *foot* and obsolete *pad* (highwayman): a thief who robs pedestrians.

Although New York City is sometimes regarded as crime-ridden, most tourists are not victims of **footpads**.

footpad

FRANGIBLE (FRAN-juh-buhl): *adj.* from Medieval Latin *frangibilis*, from Latin *fangere* (to break): capable of being broken: breakable, brittle, fragile.

The elderly woman's bones were too **frangible** to escape damage from her fall.

FRANION (FRAN-yun): *n.* origin unknown: a habitual pleasure-seeker, hedonist; a paramour; a loose woman.

Hugh Hefner, who started *Playboy* magazine, has always attracted **franions** to his famous parties.

FROTTAGE (fraw-TAZH): *n.* from French, from *frotter* (to rub): sexual gratification from rubbing one's body against another, especially in a crowded conveyance, such as an elevator, train, or bus.

Candace would always carry bags with her on the subway to shield her from weirdos interested in **frottage**.

FRUSTRANEOUS (fruh-STRAY-nee-us): *adj.* from Latin *frustra* (in vain): vain, useless, ineffectual, unprofitable.

Many people give up trying to lose weight after many **frustraneous** attempts.

FULMINATION (FUHL-mi-**NAY**-shin): *n.* from Latin *fulminatus*, past participle of *fulminare* (to lightning): a loud, violent explosion, either a literal one (such as the detonation of a bomb) or a figurative one (such as a vehement denunciation).

fulmination

The teacher's **fulminations** against plagiarism frightened some students.

FUNAMBULIST (fyoo-NAM-byu-list): *n.* from Latin *funambulus* (funambulist), from *funis* (rope) and *-ambulus*, from *ambulare* (to walk): ropewalker; a tightrope walker.

A **funambulist** can attract even more of a crowd than usual if he walks the rope without a safety net.

FURIBUND (**FYOO**-ruh-BUHND): *adj.* from Latin *furibundus*, from *furere* (to be mad, rage): frenzied, raging.

Elmo became **furibund** when a colleague questioned his competence.

FUSTIGATE (**FUHS**-ti-GAYT): *v.* from *fustigare*, from Latin *fustis* (club) and *-igare* (akin to *agere*, to drive, act, do): i. to beat with a club; cudgel; ii. to criticize harshly.

If salespeople want to be successful, they need to praise people, not **fustigate** them.

GABERLUNZIE (gab-ur-LUN-zee): *n.* origin unknown: a wandering beggar; also, a Scottish beggar licensed to accept alms or public charity.

We gave the **gaberlunzie** a few bucks for food.

GAMMER (GAM-ur): *n.* from probably a contraction of *godmother*: an old woman.

The **gammer** was remarkably fit for her age.

gasconade

GASCONADE (gas-KUH-NAYD): *n.* from French *gasconnade*, from *gasconner* (to boast): boastfulness; bravado.

Football players are given to **gasconade** when they guarantee a victory.

GELID (JEL-id): *adj.* from Latin *gelidus* (icy, cold): extremely cold; icy.

Beatrice suffered from hypothermia after she fell into the **gelid** waters of the Atlantic.

GENECLEXIS (JEN-i-KLEK-sis): *n.* from Greek *genos* (sex, birth, origin) and *eklegein* (to select): selecting a marriage partner on the basis of physical appearance without regard for intellect or character.

People whose attachment to physical appearance leads them to **geneclexis** often have marriages that end quickly.

GLABELLA (gluh-BEL-uh): *n.* from Latin, feminine of *glabellus* (hairless, smooth), from *glaber* (bald): the flat area of the forehead between the eyebrows.

The focal point of much meditation can be found within the **glabella**.

GLABROUS (GLAY-br<u>us</u>): *adj.* from Latin *glaber* (bald): i. having no hairs or projections; ii. smooth or bald as in glabrous scalps or glabrous leaves.

Japanese women are used to seeing men with **glabrous** chests.

glabrous

GLEET (gleet): *n.* from Middle English *glet* (slime), from Middle French *glete*, from Latin *glittus* (sticky): i. a chronic inflammation of a bodily orifice in people or animals usually accompanied by an abnormal discharge from the orifice (nasal *gleet*); ii. the discharge itself (as in the urethral mucous discharge in gonorrhea).

Because of Mark's severe cold, some of his nasal **gleet** landed on his shirt.

GLIRIFORM (GLEER-<u>u</u>-form): *adj.* from Latin *glir-*, *glis* (dormouse): resembling a rodent.

The vampire in the movie was depicted as having **gliri-form** teeth.

GOBEMOUCHE (gohb-MOOSH): *n.* from French, from *gober* (to gulp down, swallow) and *mouche* (fly), from Latin *musca*: i. a credulous person; ii. a person who believes everything he hears.

When the comedian and social critic compared believing in Jesus to believing in Santa Claus, he seemed to imply that Christianity is only for **gobemouches**.

GRAMINIVOROUS (GRAM-i-**NIV**-or-us): *adj.* from Latin *gramen* (grass) and *-vorous* (eating, feeding on): feeding on grass.

Cows are good examples of **graminivorous** animals, as anyone knows who has seen them graze.

GRANDILOQUENCE (gran-DIL-u-kwints): *n.* from Latin *grandiloquus,* from *grandis* (great) and *loqui* (to speak): pompous or bombastic speech or expression.

The author and lexicographer Samuel Johnson was known for his **grandiloquence**.

GRAPHOSPASM (GRAF-oh-**SPAZ'M**): *n.* from Greek *grapho-* (writing) and *spasm*: writer's cramp.

Because Thomas Jefferson wrote literally thousands of letters, sometimes writing for hours at a time, one wonders how often he experienced **graphospasms**.

GRAVEOLENT (gra-VEE-uh-lint): *adj.* from Latin *graveolens*, from *gravis* (heavy) and *olens*, present participle of *olero* (to smell): having a rank, repulsive odor.

The young children became nauseated when they approached the **graveolent** swamp.

GRAVID (GRAV-id): *adj.* from Latin *gravidus* (pregnant), from *gravis* (heavy): pregnant.

The obviously **gravid** woman needed to buy maternity clothes.

GRESSORIAL (gre-SOHR-ee-uhl): *adj.* from Latin *gressus*, past participle of *gradi* (to step, go): adapted for walking.

Most birds have **gressorial** feet, enabling them to walk.

GRIFFONAGE (GREE-fuh-**NAZH**): *n.* from Middle French *grifouner* (to scribble): sloppy or illegible handwriting.

Medical doctors, known for their **griffonage**, sometimes take classes to help them write more neatly.

GRIMALKIN (gruh-MAHL-kuhn): *n.* from alteration of *graymalkin*, from *gray* and *malkin*, from name *Maud* : i. cat, especially an elderly queen; ii. an old and usually cantankerous or otherwise unpleasant woman.

grimalkin

Our Tabby was a twenty-year-old **grimalkin**.

GRIMTHORPE (GRIM-thorp): *v.* from Sir Edmund Beckett, first Baron *Grimthorpe*, who was an English lawyer and architect who lived principally in the nineteenth century and who was severely criticized for the way in which he tried to restore St. Albans Cathedral in England: to remodel (an ancient building) without proper knowledge or care to retain its original quality and character.

We couldn't believe that the city let an inexperienced architect **grimthorpe** the historic building.

GROBIAN (GROH-bee'n): *n.* from German, after *Grobian*, a fictional patron saint of vulgar people, from Medieval Latin (*Sanctus*) *Grobianus*, from Middle High German *grob-*, *grop* (coarse, vulgar), from Old High German *gerob*, *grob* (thick, coarse) and Latin *-ianus* (ian): a crude, sloppy, and often buffoonish person.

The actor Jack Black played a **grobian** in the 2002 movie *Orange County*.

GYNARCHY (GY-nahr-kee, JIN-nahr-kee): *n.* from Greek *gyn-* (woman) and *-archy* (rule): government by women.

Many feminists are not agitating for **gynarchy**, only equality.

HABILE (HAB-´l): *adj.* from French, from Latin *habilis* (handy, manageable, apt, fit): able, adroit, skillful.

Eye surgeons are known for the **habile** use of their hands.

HAGIOLATRY (HAG-ee-**AHL**-uh-tree, HAY-jee-**AHL**-uh-tree): *n.* from Greek-derived *hagi-* (sacred, holy) and *latreia* (service, worship): the invocation or worship of saints.

hagiolatry

The young man's praise for his sports idol bordered on **hagiolatry**.

HAUTEUR (hoh-TUR): *n.* from French *haut* (high, proud): an assumption of superiority; arrogant or condescending manner.

The famous actor's attitude of entitlement often expressed itself in his **hauteur**.

HEBETUDE (**HEB**-uh-TOOD): *n.* from Late Latin *hebetudo*, from *hebere* (to be dull): the absence of mental alertness or physical sensitivity: dullness, lethargy.

The Jerry Springer Show often has slow-witted guests who don't realize that the show exploits their **hebetude**.

HELIOLATER (HEE-lee-**AHL**-uh-tur): *n.* from Greek-derived *heli-* (sun) and *–latry, latreia* (service, worship): sun-worshiper.

Although ancient sun-worshipers had religious ceremonies governing their sun-worship, contemporary **heliolaters** worship the sun by basking in it.

HETEROGAMOSIS (HET-ur-oh-ga-**MOH**-sis): *n.* from Greek *hetero-*, *heteros* (other, different) and *gamos* (marriage) and *-osis* (a state or condition, usually unfavorable): marriage in which the partners are seriously mismatched.

It was hardly surprising that actress Julia Roberts soon divorced singer Lyle Lovett, since the marriage was widely regarded as a **heterogamosis**.

HIEMAL (HY-uh-muhl): *adj.* from Latin *hiemalis*, from *hiems* (winter): of or relating to winter: wintry.

Because we had a typical **hiemal** day, we wore our heavy coats.

hiemal

HIRUDINOID (hi-ROO-d̲i-noyd): *adj.* from Latin *hirudo* (leech) and English *-oid* (resembling): like a leech.

The man regarded bankers as **hirudinoid**, sucking the blood from people needing to borrow money.

HISTRIO (**HIS**-tree-OH): *n.* from Latin for actor or player: actor.

Had James Dean lived longer, he would probably have been one of the greatest **histrios** of his generation.

HOBBLEDEHOY (**HAHB**-uhl-dee-HOY): *n.* origin unknown: a gawky adolescent boy.

The **hobbledehoy** was so clumsy that he knocked over the pitcher of lemonade in the kitchen.

HORRIPILATION (haw-RIP-uh-**LAY**-sh<u>i</u>n): *n.* from Latin *horripilare* (to bristle with hairs), from *horrere* (to tremble) and *pilare* (to grow hair): the bristling of body hair, as from fear or cold; goose bumps.

The nurse explained to the girl that the tingling she was feeling was **horripilation**.

HORTATORY (**HAWR**-tuh-TAWR/TOHR-ee): *adj.* from Late Latin *hortatorius*, from Latin *hortatus*, past participle of *hortari* (to exhort): marked by exhortation or strong urging.

A good football coach should know how to deliver an effective **hortatory** speech.

HUMICUBATE (hyoo-MIK-yuh-bayt): *v.* from Latin *humus* (earth, ground) and *cubitus* (reclined): to lie prone or prostrate, especially in prayer or penitence; to lie still, as in prayer.

Jonathan would often **humicubate** during his quiet time, so it was difficult to tell whether he was praying or sleeping.

HYALINE (HY-uh-lin): *adj.* from Greek *hyalos* (transparent stone, glass): resembling glass, as in translucence or transparency.

When the professor accused his student of "**hyaline** mendacity," the student didn't realize he was being called a transparent liar.

HYMENEAL (HY-muh-**NEE**-uhl): *adj.* from Latin *hymenaeus* (marriage, wedding song): of, or relating to marriage.

Alyssa was delighted to receive many **hymeneal** gifts shortly after her wedding.

HYMENORRHEXIS (HY-men-uh-**REK**-sis): *n.* from Greek *hymen* (membrane) and *orexis* (appetite, desire): the act of deflowering a virgin: devirginization.

Some male adolescents regard each act of **hymenorrhexis** as a conquest.

HYPAETHRAL (hy-PEE-thruhl): *adj.* from Latin *hypaethrus* (in the open air), from Greek *hypaithros*, from *hypo-*, *hupo* (under) and *aithēr* (sky, air): wholly or partly open to the sky.

After the hurricane, Amanda's house, like some ancient temples, was **hypaethral**.

HYPERGAMY (hy-PUR-guh-mee): *n.* from Greek *hyper-* (beyond, over, above) and *gamos* (marriage): marrying someone at or above one's social station.

The peasant girl was proud of her **hypergamy**, since her marriage to the prince gave her many advantages.

HYPERMIMIA (HY-pur-**MIM**-ee-uh): *n.* from Greek *hyper-* (hyper, over, above) and *mimikos* (imitative): waving or gesticulating with hands while talking.

hypermimia

Ronaldo's **hypermimia** is so pronounced that he would have trouble talking if his hands were tied.

HYPNOPOMPIC (HIP-noh-**PAHM**-pik): *adj.* from Greek-derived *hypn-* (sleep) and *pomp-*, from *pompē* (act of sending, escort, procession): i. dispelling sleep; ii. pertaining to the fuzzy, semiconscious state between sleep and wakefulness.

After studying for hours, Deborah was in a **hypnopompic** state.

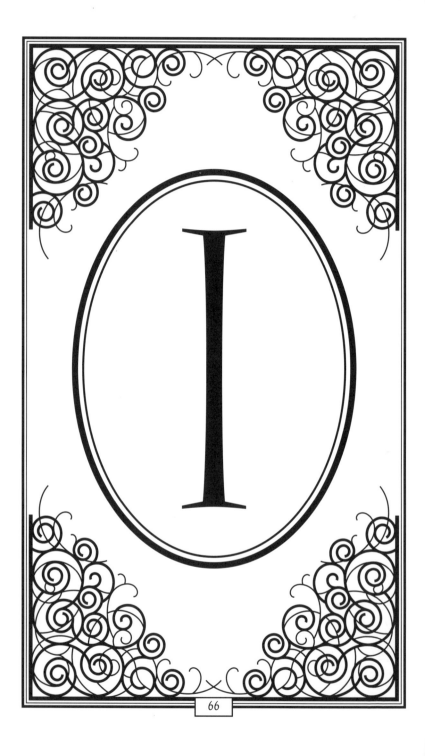

IDIOPATHIC (id-ee-uh-PATH-ik): *adj.* from New Latin *idiopathia* (primary disease), from Greek *idiopatheia*, from *idios* (one's own, personal) and *-patheia*, from *paschein* (to experience, suffer): i. peculiar to an individual; ii. *of diseases*: arising from an obscure or unknown cause.

The man's **idiopathic** associations with the old song caused him to cry whenever he heard it.

ILLEISM (IL-ee-IZ'M): *n.* from Latin *ille* (he, that one, that) and English *-ism*: excessive use of the pronoun he, especially in reference to oneself; the habit of speaking of oneself in the third person.

Although people can bore others by constantly talking about "I" and "me," they can be just as irritating by engaging in **illeism**, revealing a more subtle self-absorption.

ILLTH (ILTH): *n.* from *ill* and *-th* (as in *wealth*): poverty.

Appalachia is an area known for its **illth**.

illth

IMMUND (i-MUHND): *adj.* from Latin *immundus*, from *in-* (not) and *mundus* (clean): unclean, filthy.

Some people's homes are so **immund** that those who clean them require special facial masks for protection against germs and debris.

IMPAVID (im-PAV-id): *adj.* from Latin *impavidus*, from *in-* (not) and *pavidus* (fearful): not afraid; fearless.

Only an **impavid** boxer would laugh while entering the ring to fight Mike Tyson.

IMPROBITY (im-PROH-bi-tee): *n.* from Latin *improbitas* (wickedness, dishonesty), from *improbus* (bad, dishonest): lack of integrity or rectitude; dishonesty.

If people are to be extremely successful in sales, it is best for them to believe in their products or services and to avoid insincerity or **improbity**.

INCONDITE (in-KAHN-dit): *adj.* from Latin *inconditus* (confused, disorderly): i. badly organized, unpolished (used especially of language); ii. lacking in manners.

The professor was a maladroit writer, constantly producing **incondite** prose.

INOSCULATE (in-**AHS**-kyuh-LAYT): *v.* from Latin *osculare* (to provide with an opening): to make continuous or blend.

The movie was a historical narrative designed to **inosculate** the past and present.

INSTAURATION (inz-staw-RAY-shin): *n.* from Latin *instauratus*, past participle of *instaurare* (to renew, restore): restoration after decay, lapse, or dilapidation.

After the **instauration** of John's home, he threw a party.

INTENERATE (in-**TEN**-uh-RAYT): *v.* from *in-* and Latin *tener* (tender, sensitive): to soften.

The cook soaked the meat in a special liquid to **intenerate** it.

INVIGILATE (in-**VIJ**-uh-LAYT): *v.* from Latin *invigilatus*, past participle of *invigilare*, from *in-* and *vigilare* (to watch): to proctor an examination.

The teacher wanted a graduate student to **invigilate** her undergraduate exams.

IPSEDIXITISM (IP-si-**DIK**-si-tiz'm): *n.* from Latin *ipse dixit* (he himself has said [it]): unsupported dogmatic assertion or assertiveness.

Members of the jury wanted convincing evidence and no amount of **ipsedixitism** by the lawyer could cover up the fact that there was none.

IRENIC (eye-REN-ik): *adj.* from Greek *eirēnikos*, from *eirēnē* (peace): promoting peace; conciliatory.

Shaking people's hands was originally an **irenic** gesture to show that people were unarmed.

irenic

IRREFRAGABLE (i-REF-ruh-guh-buhl): *adj.* from Late Latin *irrefragabilis*, from Latin *in-* (not) and *refragari* (to oppose): impossible to refute or controvert; indisputable.

> The jury who acquitted Michael Jackson of child molestation charges did not regard the evidence against him as **irrefragable**.

ISAGOGE (**EYE**-suh-GOH-jee): *n.* from Greek *eisagōgē*, from *eisagein* (to introduce): a scholarly introduction to a branch of study or research.

> The authors T.H. Huxley and Isaac Asimov were known for producing **isagoges** for scientific disciplines.

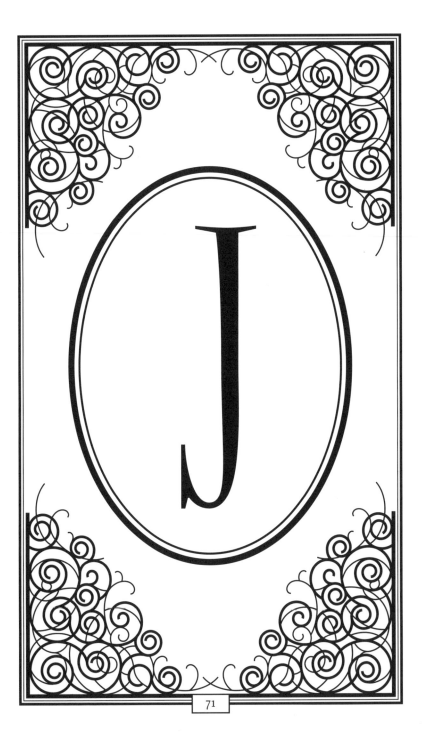

JACKANAPES (JAK-uh-NAYPS): *n.* from Middle English *Jack Napis, Jac Napes*, a nickname of William de la Pole, fourth earl and first duke of Suffolk (1396–1450): a conceited or impudent person.

jackanapes

President Truman regarded General MacArthur as a brilliant but egocentric **jackanapes**.

JACTATION (jak-TAY-shin): *n.* from Latin *jactatio* (a tossing), from *jactatus*, past participle of *jactare* (to toss or jerk the body about): boastful display or declaration.

The football player's touchdown dance was a **jactation** that annoyed the opposing team.

JACTITATE (JAK-ti-tayt): *v.* from Late Latin *jactitatus*, past participle of *jactitare*, from Latin *jactare* (to toss or jerk the body about): to toss or jerk the body about.

Abraham would **jactitate** so fitfully while trying to sleep that his wife, Elizabeth, found it impossible to rest.

JEJUNATOR (JEE-joo-nay-tur): *n.* from Latin *jejunus* (hungry) and English *-tor* (signifying an agent): a person who fasts.

Karen said that she is a **jejunator** for reasons of health rather than religious practice.

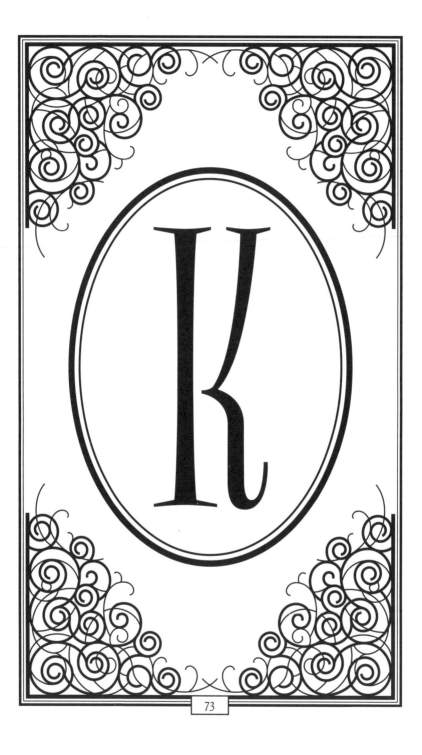

KAKIDROSIS (KAK-i-**DROH**-sis): *n.* from Greek *kakos* (bad, harmful) and *-idrosis*, from *hydros* (sweat): smelly perspiration.

When people with unbalanced diets sweat profusely, they sometimes produce **kakidrosis**.

KAKISTOCRACY (KAK-i-**STAHK**-ruh-see): *n.* from Greek *kakistos*, superlative of *kakos* (bad) and *-cracy* (rule): government by the worst people.

Plato thought that democratic government was a form of mob rule by a rabble-rousing **kakistocracy**.

KALOLOGY (kuh-LAHL-uh-jee): *n.* from Greek *kallos* (beauty) and *-logy* (study of): the study of beauty: aesthetics.

kalology

Whether beauty is an objective feature of things or at least partly a function of human perception is a question for **kalology**.

KALOPSIA (kuh-LAHP-see-uh): *n.* from Greek *kallos* (beauty) and *opsis* (sight, appearance): the delusion that things are more beautiful than they are.

People in love often have optimistic distortions in perception so that they are prone to experience **kalopsia**.

KATABASIS (kuh-TAB-uh-suhs): *n.* from Greek *katabasis* (descent), from *katabainein* (to go down): a marching down or back, especially in a military retreat.

> Some people think that the **katabasis** of inadequately protected American troops in Somalia and Lebanon emboldened terrorists to later attack various American interests.

KATABATIC (KAT-uh-**BAT**-ik): *adj.* from Greek *katabatikos* (of descent), from *katabatos* (descending): of or relating to a cold flow of air traveling downward.

> We were a little chilly because of the **katabatic** winds.

KOROPHILIA (KOR-uh-**FIL**-ee-uh): *n.* from Greek *koros* (boy, lad) and *philia* (attachment, fondness, attraction): attraction to a male younger than oneself.

> Because actress Demi Moore is much older than her husband Ashton Kutcher, some observers have ascribed **korophilia** to her.

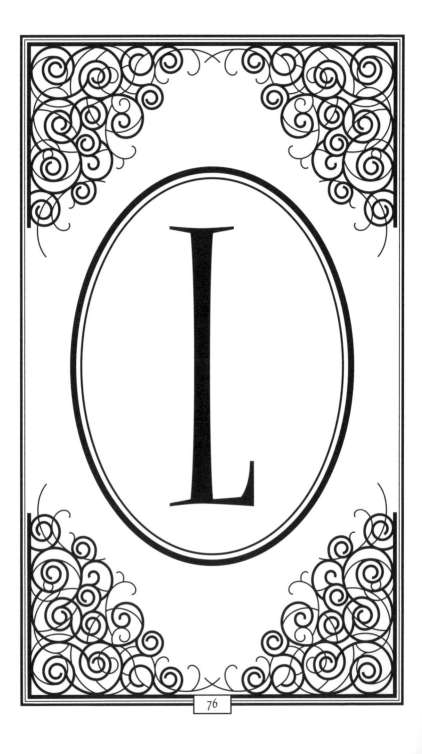

LABROSE (LAB-rohs): *adj.* from Latin *labrum* (lip) and *-ose* (having the quality of, usually denoting fullness): having full lips.

> Anyone who has seen the lips of the rock star Steven Tyler can readily see that he is **labrose**.

LACUSTRINE (luh-KUHS-truhn): *adj.* from Latin *lacus* (lake): of, relating to, formed in, living in, or growing in lakes.

> We pointed out that the fish they were eating was not found in salt water but was **lacustrine**.

LAGAN (LAG-uhn): *n.* from Middle French *lagan*, *lagand*, or Medieval Latin *laganum* (debris washed up from the sea, the right to possess such debris): goods thrown into the sea with a buoy attached so that they can be found again.

> The cargo floating in the sea was definitely **lagan** and not flotsam.

LANUGINOUS (luh-NOO-juh-nuhs): *adj.* from Latin *lanuginosus*, from *lanugo* (down of plants or the beard): covered with soft, short hair; downy.

> We enjoyed petting the dog's **lanuginous** coat.

LAODICEAN (lay-AHD-uh-**SEE**-in): *adj.* from *Laodicea*, ancient city in Asia Minor whose Christian inhabitants were known for their lukewarm attitude toward their faith: lukewarm or indifferent in religion or politics.

Kimberly was so passionate about political issues that she became upset over her husband's **Laodicean** attitude.

LAPACTIC (luh-PAK-tik): *adj.* from Greek *lapaktikos*, from probably *lapaktos*, from Greek *lapassein* (to empty): cathartic, laxative.

When Edmund came out of the closet, he found it stressful at first but eventually **lapactic**.

LAPIDATE (**LAP**-i-DAYT): *v.* from Latin *lapidatus*, past participle of *lapidare* (to stone): to stone to death.

It is reported that Jesus told the men who were preparing to **lapidate** a woman accused of adultery that they should throw the stones only if they were free of sin.

LARDACEOUS (lar-DAY-shus): *adj.* probably from New Latin *lardaceus*, from Latin *lardum* (fat pork): resembling lard.

The vegetarian looked at the plate of spare ribs and told his host that he does not eat "**lardaceous** crap."

LATERITIOUS (**LAT**-uh-RISH-uhs): *adj.* from Latin *latericius* (made of brick): brick-red.

Toulouse, France, is known as "the Pink City" because of its many **lateritious** buildings made of old bricks.

LATRATE (LAY-trayt): *v.* from Latin *latratus*, past participle of *latrare* (to bark): to bark like a dog.

Bryn was embarrassed when her husband Abe began to **latrate** at the formal dinner.

LAUREATE (LAWR-ee-ayt): *v.* from Middle English *laureat* (crowned with laurel as a distinction), from Latin *laureatus* (crowned with laurel), from *laurea* (laurel wreath): to crown with or as if with a laurel wreath for excellence or achievement.

In the 1960s, Americans often **laureated** astronauts.

LEGIST (LEE-jist): *n.* from Middle French *legiste*, from Old French, from Medieval Latin *legista*, from Latin *lex* (law): a specialist in law.

legist

The famous **legist** was often called on to explain Supreme Court rulings.

LEIOTRICHOUS (LY-uh-TRI-kuhs): *adj.* from New Latin *leiotrichi*: having straight, smooth hair.

Although the man who committed the crime had curly hair, the original suspect was **leiotrichous**.

LENTIC (LEN-tik): *adj.* from Latin *lentus* (slow, calm, sluggish): of, or relating to, or living in still waters (as lakes, ponds, swamps).

Stephanie preferred the **lentic** calm of the lake to the roar of the ocean.

LENTIGINOUS (**LEN**-TIJ-uh-nuhs): *adj.* from Latin *lentiginosus*, from *lentigo* (lentil): freckled.

Howdy Doody was a famous **lentiginous** TV puppet, reportedly with forty-eight freckles, each representing a state in the 1950s.

LEPTODACTYLOUS (**LEP**-tuh-DAK-tuh-luhs): *adj.* from Greek *leptos* (fine, thin) and *dactylos* (finger, dactyl): having slender toes.

Murray's foot fetish led him to beaches and swimming pools to eye **leptodactylous** women.

LEPTORRHINIAN (LEP-tuh-**RIN**-ee-in): *adj.* from French *leptorrhin*, from Greek-derived *lepto-* (thin, delicate) and *-rrhin* (nose, snout, beak): having a long, narrow nose.

leptorrhinian

A **leptorrhinian** woman can be attractive if her face is long enough for her nose.

LEPTOSOME (**LEP**-tuh-SOHM): *n.* from Greek *leptos* (fine, thin) and *sōma* (body): a person with a slender, thin, or frail body.

Because Sherwood was a **leptosome**, his mother did not want him playing football.

LEXIPHANICISM (LEKS-i-**FAN**-i-siz'm): *n.* from the character *Lexiphanes* (word-shower) in Lucian's dialogue *Lexiphanes*: pretentious linguistic expressions.

> W.C. Fields would often play characters given to **lexiphanicism**, as when one character described a beverage as "liquid saturnalia."

LIBIDOCORIA (li-BID-uh-**KUR**-ee-uh): *n.* from Latin *libido* (sex drive), Greek *a-* (without), and Greek *koros* (satiety): uncontrollable and insatiable sexual desire.

> Because of Hugh's **libidocoria**, he was never completely satisfied by his numerous sexual encounters.

LICKERISH (LIK-uhr-ish): *adj.* from Middle English *likerous*, perhaps from Old French *lecheor*, from *lechier* (to lick, to live in debauchery): i. lascivious, lecherous; ii. greedy, desirous.

> James Bond was a suave but **lickerish** man known for his sexual appetite.

LICKSPITTLE (**LIK**-SPIT-'l): *n.* from *lick* and *spittle*: an abject parasite or toady.

> Dictators like to surround themselves with **lickspittles**.

LIMACINE (LIM/LYM-uh-seen): *adj.* from New Latin *limacinus*, from Latin *limac-*, *limax* (slug): of, relating to, or resembling a slug.

> The **limacine** child was called a slowpoke.

LIMICOLOUS (ly-MIK-uh-l<u>u</u>s): *adj.* from Latin *limus* (mud, slime) and *-colous* (dwelling in): living in mud.

When Molly had discovered her son playing in the mud, she called him a "**limicolous** fool."

LIMITROPHE (**LIM**-uh-TROHF): *adj.* from Late Latin *limitrophus* (set apart to furnish subsistence to troops stationed on the frontiers), irregular from Latin *limes* (boundary, limit) and Greek *trophos* (feeder): adjacent, neighboring.

Skirmishes between **limitrophe** powers, such as Russia and China, have been common throughout history.

LINCTUS (LINK-tuhs): *n.* from Latin, past participle of *lingere* (to lick): a cough syrup.

The **linctus**, though bitter, soothed Barry's throat and reduced his coughing.

LINGUA (LING-gwuh): *n.* from Latin *lingua* (tongue, language): tongue or tonguelike organ.

A **lingua** protruded from the llama's mouth and licked Caleb's hand.

LIPOTHYMIC (LY-puh-**THIM**-ik): *adj.* from Late Latin *lipothymia*, from Greek *lipothymein* (to faint): tending to faint.

The students were used to reading about **lipothymic** Victorian heroines who had trouble remaining conscious when excited.

LIPPITUDE (LIP-i̱-t(y)ood): *n.* from Latin *lippitus*, past participle of *lippire* (to have sore eyes): soreness of the eyes.

Kristin's **lippitude** was caused by reading all night.

LOGOLEPT (LAHG-uh-lept): *n.* from Greek *logos* (word, discourse) and Greek suffix *-lepsia* (seizure): a person who has seizures about words.

The **logolept** became so disturbed by the speaker's ungrammatical speech that he fainted.

LOGOMANIAC (LAHG-uh-**MAY**-nee-ak): *n.* from Greek *logos* (word, discourse) and *mania* (madness, obsession): a person obsessed with words.

A confirmed **logomaniac**, Christine would constantly carry dictionaries with her.

logomaniac

LOGORRHEA (LAHG-uh-**REE**-uh): *n.* from New Latin, from Greek *logos* (word, discourse) and *-rrhea* (flow, stream): pathologically excessive and often incoherent talkativeness.

Few things are as exasperating as trying to follow the train of thought of a person suffering from **logorrhea**.

LONGANIMITY (LAHNG-guh-**NIM**-i̱-tee): *n.* from Late Latin *longanimitas*, from *longanimis* (patient): calmness in the face of suffering and adversity; forbearance.

The political prisoner bore the verbal abuse and torture with **longanimity**.

LONGUEUR (lawng-GUR): *n.* from French *longueur* (length), from Old French *longour*, from *lonc, long* (long), from Latin *longus* (long): a dull and tedious passage or section, as of a book or play—often used in plural.

Some books, despite their **longueurs**, can still be informative.

LOTIC (LOHD-ik, LOH-tik): *adj.* from Latin *lotus* (action of washing or bathing), from *lautus, lotus*, past participle of *lavere* (to wash): of, relating to, or living in actively moving water (as in stream currents or waves).

Matthew found the **lotic** sounds around his beachfront property calming.

LOUCHE (loosh): *adj.* from Old French *losche* (squint-eyed), feminine of *lois*, from Latin *luscus* (blind in one eye): of questionable taste or morality.

The rock star Madonna became popular partly because she succeeded in shocking people by her **louche** behavior.

LUCUBRATOR (**LOO**-kyoo-BRAY-tur): *n.* from Latin *lucubratus*, past participle of *lucubrare* (to work by lamplight, compose by night): one who writes scholarly material.

A professor who wants a full-time position at a major research university had better be a prolific **lucubrator**, with numerous articles to his or her credit.

LUCULENT (LOO-kyuh-luhnt): *adj.* from Middle English, from Latin *luculentus* (full of light), from *luc-*, *lux* (light): i. transparent; ii. clear in thought or expression.

Sir Francis Bacon, one of Shakespeare's contemporaries, was known for his **luculent** essays.

LUDDITE (LUH-dyt): *n.* from Ned *Ludd*, early-nineteenth-century Englishman who went about smashing up stocking frames (mechanized looms): i. a member of a group of early-nineteenth-century English workmen engaged in attempting to prevent the use of labor-saving machinery by destroying it; ii. any person who is firmly opposed to technology, especially innovative technology.

The Unabomber was not only a brilliant mathematician but also a **Luddite** who killed people in the name of saving humanity from modern technology.

LUNULA (LOON-yuh-luh): *n.* from Latin *lunula* (diminutive of *luna*, moon): the half-moon or crescent-shaped pale area at the base of the fingernail or toenail.

One of Sarah's cuticles was so large that it covered most of her **lunula**.

LUPANAR (loo-PAY/PAH-nuhr): *n.* from Latin *lupa* (prostitute), literally, she-wolf, feminine of *lupus*: house of prostitution: bordello.

The mayor was not re-elected because his frequent visits to the town **lupanar** became public knowledge.

MACROGRAPHY (ma-KRAW-gruh-fee): *n.* from Greek *makros* (long) and *graphein* (to write): i. examination of an object with the unaided eye; ii. abnormally large handwriting, sometimes indicating a nervous disorder.

> After seeing Bertha's **macrography**, her teacher wondered whether she was immature, unintelligent, or psychologically disturbed.

MACROTOUS (muh-KROH-tus): *adj.* from Greek *makros* (long) and Greek *ōt, ous* (ear): having large ears.

> Many people laughed when they heard the **macrotous** billionaire H. Ross Perot describe himself as "all ears."

MALEDICENT (MAL-e-DY-sint): *adj.* from Latin *maledicere* (to speak evil): given to vicious, abusive speech.

> The meek man decided to divorce his **maledicent** wife for his peace of mind.

MALISON (MAL-uh-suhn): *n.* from Middle English *malisoun*, from Old French, from Latin *maledictio*, from *maledictus*, past participle of *maledicere* (to speak ill): a curse.

> John hated Paul so much that he called down a **malison** on him.

MALVERSATION (MAL-vur-SAY-shin): *n.* from Middle French, from *malverser* (to misbehave), from Old French, from Latin *male versari*, from *male* (wrongly, ill) and *versari* (to behave, conduct oneself): corruption in a position.

Spiro Agnew, Richard Nixon's vice president, had to resign because of his **malversation**.

MANSUETUDE (**MAN**-swuh-TOOD): *n.* from Middle English, from Latin *mansuetudo*, from *mansuetus* (tame): meekness, tameness, gentleness.

The librarian was a kind, self-effacing man known for his **mansuetude**.

MANTIC (MAN-tik): *adj.* from Greek *mantikos* (prophetic), from *mantis* (seer, prophet): pertaining to the attempt to foretell the future; prophetic.

Many skeptics doubt whether the famous seer Edgar Cayce had **mantic** powers.

MARTEXT (MAHR-tekst): *n.* from English *mar* and *text*: a blundering preacher, especially one who stumbles through a sermon.

When the **martext** described Saint Paul as the most beloved of the twelve disciples, he was asked to find a new church.

MASTILAGNIA (MAS-ti-**LAG**-nee-uh): *n.* from Greek *mastigos* (whip), from *mastix* (whip) and *lagneia* (lust): sexual pleasure derived from being whipped.

We didn't learn about Merwin's **mastilagnia** until we saw his wife carrying a whip into the motel.

MATTOID (MAT-oyd): *n.* from Latin *mattus* (stupid, drunk) and Greek *-oide*, *-oid* (like): i. a person degenerate or half-mad from birth; ii. a person with a congenitally abnormal brain.

The **mattoid** was institutionalized after he tortured several of the neighbors' cats.

MATUTINAL (muh-T(Y)OO-ti-nul): *adj.* from Latin *matutinus* (of the morning): i. of, relating to, or occurring in the morning; ii. early.

People who live and work on dairy farms are used to **matutinal** chores.

MEMORITER (muh-MOR-uh-tur): *adv.* from Latin *memor* (with a good memory): by or from memory; by heart.

The young child learned **memoriter** the alphabet.

MENTUM (MEN-tuhm): *n.* from Latin for chin: chin.

mentum

The boxer landed a right hook to his opponent's **mentum**.

MERDIVOROUS (mur-DIV-ur-us): *adj.* from Latin *merda* (excrement) and English suffix *-vorous* (eat): feeding on excrement.

The scarab is a good example of a **merdivorous** beetle.

MESOTHETIC (**ME**-zuh-THED-ik): *adj.* from Greek *mesos* (middle) and *thetikos* (of placing): being in a middle position: intermediate.

> Because of Reggie's **mesothetic** score on his SAT, he was unable to enter Princeton.

METEMPSYCHOSIS (muh-TEM-si-**KOH**-sis/MET-uhm-sy-**KOH**-sis): *n.* from Greek *metempsychōsis,* from *metempsychousthai* (to transmigrate): reincarnation.

> Before Nina said that she used to be an English princess, we had no idea that she believed in **metempsychosis**.

MINIMUS (MIN-u̱-mu̱s): *n.* from Latin for smallest or least: i. a being of the smallest size: a tiny creature; ii. the little finger or toe.

> The pitcher had to be removed from the game after he sprained his left **minimus**.

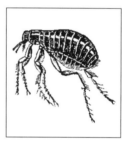

minimus

MISOGAMY (mis-AHG-uh-mee): *n.* from Greek *misos* (hate) and *gamos* (marriage): hatred of marriage; aversion to marriage.

> Although Warren Beatty was a bachelor for decades, he gave the lie to the accusation of **misogamy** when he got married.

MISONEISTIC (MIS-oh-nee-**IS**-tik): *adj.* from Greek *misos* (hate) and *neos* (new): hatred or intolerance of what is new or changed.

The radio talk show host insisted that people can be politically conservative without being **misoneistic**.

MOIETY (MOY-i-tee): *n.* from Middle English *moite*, from Old French *meitiet, moitie*, from Late Latin *medietas*, from Latin *medius* (middle): a half.

Each of the twins received a **moiety** of the estate.

MOME (mohm): *n.* origin unknown: a stupid doltish person; blockhead, fool.

Many intelligent actors, such as Jim Carrey, become famous at least partly because of their ability to portray **momes**.

MONDIAL (MAHN-dee-uhl): *adj.* from French *monde* (world): of, or involving a large part of the world or the entire world.

Many people argue that America's consumption of energy has **mondial** environmental consequences.

MONEPIC (MAH/MOH-nep-ik): *adj.* from Greek *monos* (one) and *epos* (word): consisting of one word or of sentences of one word.

Since Jesse was a taciturn rock star, he was expected to answer in **monepic** sentences.

MONOGENISM (muh-NAHJ-uh-niz'm): *n.* from Greek *monos* (one) and English combining form *-gen* (be born, causing, producing): the belief that the human race is descended from two persons, such as Adam and Eve.

> The evangelical Christian insisted that anyone who believes in the possibility of **monogenism** ought to entertain the possibility of the historical existence of Adam and Eve.

MONOMACHY (ma-NAHM-uh-kee): *n.* from Middle French *monomachie*, from Latin *monomachia*, from Greek *monos* (one, single, alone) and *machomai* (fight): a duel.

> Alexander Hamilton lost his life in a **monomachy** with then-vice president Aaron Burr.

monomachy

MONTEITH (mahn-TEETH): *n.* from *Monteith*, a seventeenth-century Scottish eccentric who wore a cloak with a scalloped hem: a large silver punch bowl with scalloped rim.

> When Clyde relieved himself in the **monteith** at their wedding reception, Melinda wanted to kill him.

MORTMAIN (MORT-mayn): *n.* from Middle English *mortemayne*, from Old French *mortemain*, from *morte*, feminine of *mort* (dead) and Latin *manus* (hand): the often oppressive influence of the past on the present.

Many of the hippies of the 1960s regarded themselves as rebelling against the forces of **mortmain**.

MURREY (MUHR-ee): *adj.* from Middle English *murrei*, from Old French *more*, from Latin *morum* (mulberry, blackberry): a purplish black.

When Reba wore her **murrey** outfit, she looked like a giant mulberry.

MYRMIDON (MUR-mi-dahn): *n.* from Latin *Myrmidon-, Myrmido*, from Greek *Myrmidon-, Myrmidōn*: i. one of the legendary Thessalian people accompanying Achilles to the Trojan War known for their ruthless obedience; ii. a devoted follower or servant who obeys without question or scruple.

Hitler liked having **myrmidons** under his control because he knew that they would blindly follow his commands.

MYTHOMANE (MITH-uh-mayn): *n.* from Greek *mythos* (myth) and Greek *mania* (madness, frenzy): a person who has an abnormal propensity for lying and exaggerating.

Although it is true that Al Gore has on occasion spoken falsely or inaccurately, it is probably unfair to call him a **mythomane**.

NATATION (nuh/nay-TAY-shin): *n.* from Latin *natatus*, past participle of *natare* (to swim): the action or art of swimming.

Selma learned **natation** at age six, when her parents bought the swimming pool.

NATES (NAY-teez): *n.* from Latin plural of *natis* (buttock): buttocks.

Joyce loved to wear tight jeans to show off her shapely **nates**.

NEPENTHE (nuh-PEN-thee): *n.* from Latin *nepenthes*, from Greek *nēpenthes* (banishing pain and sorrow): a drug or potion that makes one forget one's sorrows or misfortunes.

For many people, alcohol is a **nepenthe**, used temporarily to escape their problems.

NEPHALISM (NEF-uh-liz-uhn): *n.* from Middle Greek *nēphalismos* (sobriety), from Greek *nēphalios* (sober): total abstinence from alcoholic beverages.

nephalism

Although the insightful author Wayne Dyer does not condemn people for drinking alcohol, he believes that for him, **nephalism** is the best course.

NIDIFICATE (NID-i-fi-kayt): *v.* from Latin *nidificatus*, past participle of *nidificare* (to build a nest): to build a nest.

Birds do not need to go to school to learn to **nidificate**.

NIDOR (NY-dor/duhr): *n.* from Greek *knisa, knisē* (smell of burnt sacrifice): a strong smell, especially the smell of cooking or burning meat or fat.

The vegetarian was sickened by the **nidor** at the picnic barbecue.

nidor

NIMIETY (ni-MY-uh-tee): *n.* from Late Latin *nimietas*, from Latin *nimius* (too much): excess, redundancy.

The economist asserted that one reason public schools cost more to run than parochial schools is that public schools often have a **nimiety** of administrators.

NIMINY-PIMINY (NI-muh-nee-**PI**-muh-nee): *adj.* probably alteration of *namby-pamby*: affectedly refined: finicky.

The drill sergeant told the young recruit that because marines must easily adapt to all circumstances, the corps cannot tolerate **niminy-piminy** soldiers.

NITID (NID/NIT-id): *adj.* from Latin *nitidus* (shining, glittering, bright): bright, glossy, lustrous.

During the romantic evening the sky was dark, the stars were sparkling, and the moon was **nitid**.

NOCTIVAGANT (nahk-TIV-uh-g<u>i</u>nt): *adj.* from Latin *noctivagus* (night-wandering), from *noct-*, *nox* (night) and *vagus* (wandering): going about in the night; night-wandering.

The elderly couple felt apprehensive around the drunken, **noctivagant** teenagers.

NOLITION (noh-LISH-uhn): *n.* probably from French, from Middle French, from Latin *nolle* (not to will, to be unwilling): unwillingness.

Although we knew that Melvin didn't cooperate with Lucille, we didn't know whether the lack of cooperation stemmed from his ignorance of Lucille's situation or his **nolition**.

NULLIFIDIAN (nuhl-uh-FID-ee-uhn): *n.* from Latin *nullus* (not, none, no) and *fides* (faith): a religious skeptic or disbeliever.

The author H.L. Mencken regarded himself, or at least described himself, as a person completely lacking faith—a **nullifidian**.

NULLIPARA (nuh-LIP-uh-ruh): *n.* from Latin *nullus* (not, none, no) and *parere* (to produce, bring forth): a childless woman.

The young woman said that she will continue to be a **nullipara** until she meets a man she wants to marry.

NUMMIFORM (**NUHM**-uh-FORM): *adj.* from French *nummiforme*, from Latin *nummus* (coin): coin-shaped.

At the restaurant, Jason ordered some **nummiform** fried potatoes.

NYCTALOPIA (NIK-tuh-**LOH**-pee-uh): *n.* from Latin *nyctalops* (unable to see at twilight), from Greek *nyktalōp-*, *nyktalōps*, from *nykt-*, *nyct-* (night) and *alaos* (blind): i. night-blindness; ii. reduced vision in dim light or darkness.

Because of Jessica's **nyctalopia**, she would rarely drive her car at night.

OBLIVESCENCE (AHB-luh-**VES**-uhn(t)s): *n.* from Latin *obliviscor* (forget): an act or the process of forgetting.

Sometimes **oblivescence** is a coping mechanism, enabling us to rid our minds of unpleasant thoughts.

OBMUTESCENT (AHB-myoo-**TES**-int): *adj.* from Latin *obmutescere* (to become mute): becoming or keeping silent or mute.

Too many German citizens were **obmutescent** during Hitler's reign.

OBREPTITIOUS (ah-BREP-tish-uhs): *adj.* from Late Latin *obrepticius, obreptitius,* from Latin *obreptus,* past participle of *obrepere* (to creep up): done or obtained by trickery or by concealing the truth.

Many people thought that O.J. Simpson's legal defense succeeded at least partly because it was **obreptitious**.

OBVELATION (AHB-vuh-**LAY**-shin): *n.* from Late Latin *obvelare* (to cover over, hide): act of veiling or concealing.

Once an investigative journalist began to look into Maggie's past, she made herself hard to reach through **obvelation**.

OCHLOCRACY (ahk-**LAHK**-ruh-see): *n.* from Greek *ochlokratia,* from *ochlos* (crowd, mob) and *-kratia, -cracy* (rule): government by the mob: mob rule.

Unless popular rule is limited by the law or a constitution, it can produce an **ochlocracy**.

OCTOTHORPE (**AHK**-tuh-THORP): *n.* Greek-derived *okto* (eight) and *-thorpe* (from James Edward Oglethorpe): the pound sign (#).

> The operator instructed me to press the **octothorpe** on the touch pad.

ODONTALGIA (oh-dahn-TAHL-jee-uh, oh-dahn-TAHL-juh): *n.* from Greek *ondontalgeia*, from *odous, odontos* (tooth) and *algos* (pain): toothache.

> Steve's **odontalgia** prompted him to make an appointment with the dentist.

odontalgia

OECIST (EE-sist): *n.* from Greek *oikistēs*, from *oikos* (house): colonizer.

> Some Iraqis see Americans as liberators, but others see Americans as **oecists**.

OENOPHILIST (ee-NAHF-i-list): *n.* from Greek *oinos* (wine) and *philia* (love, affection): lover or connoisseur of wine.

> Frasier Crane from the TV show *Frasier* is depicted as a lover of good food and a knowledgeable **oenophilist**, capable of easily identifying a wine from one sip.

OLECRANON (oh-LEK-ruh-nahn): *n.* from Greek *ōlekranon*, from *ōlenē* (elbow) and *kranion* (head, skull): the bony tip of the elbow.

When Toby slipped and fell backwards, he landed on his left elbow and scraped his **olecranon**.

OLIGOPHRENIA (AHL-i/uh-goh-**FREE**-nee-uh): *n.* from Greek *oligos* (few, scanty) and *phren* (mind): mental deficiency: feeblemindedness.

Jill's **oligophrenia** disabled her from performing intellectually difficult tasks.

OMNIFARIOUS (AHM-ni-**FAIR**-ee-uhs): *adj.* from Latin *omnifarium* (on every side): of all kinds.

Benjamin Franklin was known for his **omnifarious** knowledge and accomplishments.

OMNILEGENT (ahm-NIL-uh-juhnt): *adj.* from Latin *omnis* (all) and *legens,* present participle of *legere* (to read): reading or having read everything: characterized by encyclopedic reading.

John Milton was so voracious a reader as to have been nearly **omnilegent**.

ONEIROCRITIC (oh-NY-ruh-**KRIT**-ik): *n.* from Greek *oneirokritikos,* from *oneiros* (dream) and *kritikos* (capable of judging): an interpreter of dreams.

Although there are books on interpreting dreams and dream symbols, it is doubtful that anyone can legitimately claim to be a scientific **oneirocritic**.

ONIOMANIA (OH-nee-uh-**MAY**-nee-uh): *n.* from Greek *ōnios* (to be bought, for sale), from *ōnos* (price) and *mania* (madness, frenzy): an uncontrollable urge to buy things.

It is usually wise never to give a person with **oniomania** a credit card.

ONYCHOPHAGY (AHN-i̱-**KAHF**-uh-jee): *n.* from Greek-derived *onycho-, onyx, -ychos* (fingernail, talon, claw) and *-phagy*, from *phagein* (to eat): chewing on one's nails.

Because Susan was nervous and highly oral, she would often resort to **onychophagy**.

OPEROSE (AHP-uh-ROHS): *adj.* from Latin *operosus* (painstaking, busy, toilsome), from *opus* (work): i. involving great labor; ii. industrious.

operose

Burt was a workaholic who prided himself on his ability to perform **operose** tasks.

OPSIGAMY (ahp-SIG-uh-mee): *n.* from Greek *opsios* (late) and *gamos* (marriage): marriage late in life.

Because Tim was unmarried until he was sixty, his **opsigamy** surprised many people.

OPSIMATH (AHP-si-math): *n.* from Greek *opsimathēs* (late in learning), from *opsios* (late) and *mathēs*, from *manthanein* (to learn): a late learner.

Friends described Debbie, who learned to read at eighty-two, as an **opsimath**.

OPTIMITY (ahp-TIM-uh-tee): *n.* from Latin *optimus* (best): the condition or fact of being best or for the best.

Kiefer's choices were good but fell short of **optimity**.

ORTHOPRAXY (OR-thuh-PRAK-see): *n.* from Greek *orthos* (straight, correct, normal) and *praxis* (doing, practice): strict adherence to the practices and doctrines of one's chosen faith.

The Orthodox Jew explained that Jewish **orthopraxy** prohibits consuming meat with dairy products.

OSTENT (ahs-TENT): *n.* from Latin *ostentus, ostentum*, from *ostendere* (to become visible, show): i. a significant sign or portent; ii. appearance, manifestation; iii. ostentation.

When Melissa began to slur her speech and to forget things, her daughter rightly viewed that behavior as an **ostent** of serious mental deterioration.

OVINE (OH-vyn): *adj.* from Latin *ovis* (sheep): like a sheep.

The radio talk show host called people 'sheeple' to suggest an **ovine** conformity.

OZOSTOMIA (OH-zah-**STOH**-mee-uh): *n.* from Greek *ozostomos* (having bad breath), from *ozo-* (bad smell) and *-stomos*, *stoma* (mouth): the condition of having bad breath; halitosis.

We let our shop teacher know our unhappiness with his **ozostomia** by leaving a bottle of mouthwash on his desk.

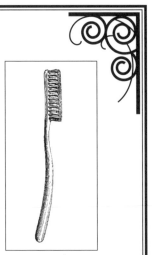

ozostomia

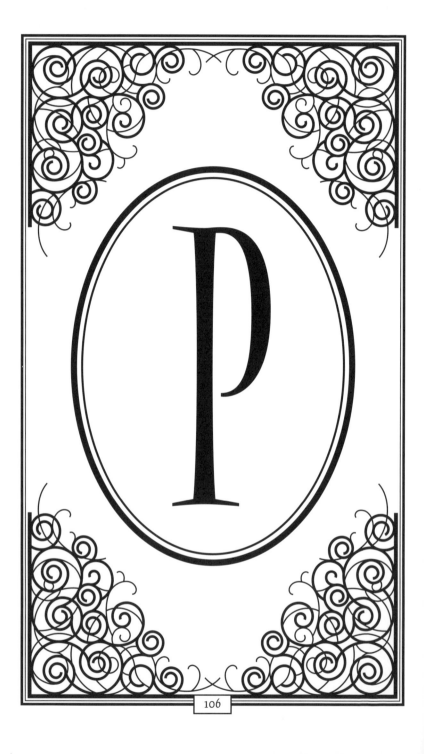

PALAESTRAL (puh-LES-truhl): *adj.* from Latin *palaestra* (place for wrestling), from Greek *palaistra*, from *palaiein* (to wrestle): pertaining to wrestling.

palaestral

Because of Alan's **palaestral** background, he was able to get the robber in an effective wrestling hold until the police arrived.

PALLADIAN (puh-LAY-dee-uhn): *adj.* from Latin *palladius* (of Pallas), from Greek *palladios*, from *Pallad-*, *Pallas* (goddess of wisdom): of, or relating to wisdom or learning.

The young man visited the guru for **palladian** discussions.

PALMARY (PAL/PAHL-muh-ree): *adj.* from Latin *palmarius* (deserving the palm): outstanding, great, best.

Because of William Faulkner's **palmary** literary achievements, he won a Nobel Prize in literature.

PALPEBRAL (pal-PEE-bruhl): *adj.* from Late Latin *palpebralis*, from *palpebra* (eyelid): of, relating to, or located on or near the eyelids.

By looking at his **palpebral** movements, we could easily tell that Bill was drowsy.

PANCRATIC (pan-KRAD/KRAT-ik): *adj.* from Greek-derived *pan-*, from *pas, pantos* (all, the whole) and *kratos* (strength, might): marked by or giving mastery of all subjects or matters.

Da Vinci revealed his **pancratic** mind in his highly varied accomplishments.

PANDICULATION (pan-DIK-yuh-**LAY**-shin): *n.* from Latin *pandiculatus*, past participle of *pandiculari* (to stretch oneself): stretching and yawning before sleep and upon waking.

The scientist asserted that **pandiculation** is an instinctive attempt to recover a balance of power between the extensor and flexor muscles.

PANDURIFORM (pan-**D(Y)UR**-uh-FORM): *adj.* from New Latin *panduriformis*, from Late Latin *pandura* (musical instrument with three strings): violin-shaped.

panduriform

We reasoned that the little boy was a violinist because he would always carry a **panduriform** case to school.

PANGLOSSIAN (pan-GLAWS-ee-uhn): *adj.* from *Pangloss*, an optimist in Voltaire's *Candide* who believed that this is the best of all possible worlds and who was a parody of the philosopher Leibniz: blindly or naively optimistic.

It is possible to be hopeful without being **Panglossian**.

PARADIDDLE (par-uh-DID-uhl): *n.* probably of imitative origin: a basic drum roll.

A good drummer needs to know how to do more than a **paradiddle**.

PARADROMIC (PAR-uh-**DRAHM/DROHM**-ik): *adj.* from Greek *paradromos*, from *para* (beside, near, by) and *dromos* (a running race): running side by side, following a parallel course.

David and Julia went to the same college, law school, and law firm and generally had **paradromic** careers.

PARAMNESIA (PAR-am-**NEE**-zhuh): *n.* from Greek *para* (beside, past, beyond) and *-mnesia* (memory): i. a condition or disorder in which one seems to remember events that never happened; ii. a condition in which people cannot recall the proper meanings of words.

If Ronald were sincere about the events he *seemed* to remember, he would have to be suffering from **paramnesia**.

PARAPH (PAR-uhf, puh-RA): *n.* from French *paraphe*, from Old French *paraffe* (abbreviated signature), from Medieval Latin *paraphus* (paragraph sign), short for *paragraphus* (paragraph): a flourish made after or below a signature, usually to prevent forgery.

It would be difficult for most forgers to imitate the wealthy man's signature because of the highly intricate **paraph**.

PARAPRAXIS (PAR-uh-**PRAK**-sis): *n.* from Greek *para* (beyond, past) and *praxis* (action): a faulty act (as a slip of the tongue or of memory).

> The executive was much more likely to commit a **parapraxis** when speaking extemporaneously than when delivering a prepared speech.

PARTURITION (PAR-tuh-**RI**-shin): *n.* from Latin *parturire* (to be in labor): the act or process of giving birth; childbirth.

> Since he wanted to see his child being born, Raymond insisted on being with his wife during her **parturition**.

PARVANIMITY (PAR-vuh-**NIM**-i-tee): *n.* from Latin *parvus* (little, small) and *-animity, anima* (soul, breath of life): pettiness; smallness of mind.

> An excessive readiness to take personal offense and a slowness to forgive are two marks of **parvanimity**.

PARVULE (PAHR-vyool): *n.* from Latin *parvulus* (very small), from *parvus* (small): a very small pill.

> The pharmacist told us that we should not judge the potency of a **parvule** simply by its size.

PECCABLE (PEK-uh-buhl): *adj.* from Latin *peccare* (to sin): i. liable or prone to sin; ii. susceptible to temptation.

> After the politician was caught embezzling money from his mistress, he asserted that we are all frail, **peccable** mortals.

PEIRASTIC (PY-ras-tik): *adj.* from Greek *peirastikos*, from *peiran* (to attempt): fitted for trial; experimental, tentative.

The **peirastic** hydrogen-powered car may eventually be mass produced.

PELARGIC (pe-LAHR-jik): *adj.* from Greek *pelargikos*, from *pelargos* (stork): of, or relating to the stork; storklike.

pelargic

The **pelargic** figure made of wood in front of Joan's house was there to notify her neighbors of her new baby.

PERICLITATE (puh-RIK-li-tayt): *v.* from Latin *periclitatus*, past participle of *periclitari*, from *periclum*, *periculum* (danger, trial): i. to imperil; ii. to be in a perilous situation.

We must protect, not **periclitate**, young children.

PERLUSTRATE (puhr-LUH-strayt): *v.* from Latin *perlustratus*, past participle of *perlustrare*, from *per-* (through) and *lustrare* (to traverse, survey, brighten): to go through and examine thoroughly.

Before buying a home, it is a good idea to **perlustrate** it.

PERNOCTATION (pur-nahk-TAY-shin): *n.* from Latin *pernocto* (to pass the night): the act of staying up all night, as in pulling an all-nighter to work, study, or party.

Jeremy's **pernoctation** enabled him to complete his term paper.

PETTIFOGGER (**PET**-uh-FAW-gur): *n.* from *petty* and obsolete English *fogger* (underhand dealer), probably from *Fugger* (a German family of merchants in the fifteenth and sixteenth centuries): a lawyer whose methods are petty, underhanded, or disreputable: shyster.

Mary needed an honest and competent lawyer, but what she got was a **pettifogger**.

PHAROS (FAR-ahs): *n.* from Greek *Pharos* (island in the bay of Alexandria, Egypt, famous for its lighthouse): a lighthouse.

Sailors were lost until they spotted the light from a **pharos**.

PHATIC (FAT-ik): *adj.* from Greek *phatos* (spoken), from *phanai* (to speak): of, relating to, or being speech used to share feelings or to establish a sociable mood rather than to communicate ideas or information: pertaining to small talk.

pharos

Asking people one barely knows how they are is not usually a request for in-depth information but rather **phatic** communication, designed to make people feel good.

PHILOPROGENEITY (FIL-oh-PROH-ji-**NEE**-i-tee):
n. from Greek-derived *phil-*, *phileo* (love, regard with affection) and Latin *progenies* (progeny): i. love of offspring; ii. producing many children.

> Allison expressed her **philoprogeneity** in her everyday acts of kindness on behalf of her children.

PHILOSOPHASTER (fi-**LAHS**-uh-FAS-tur): *n.* from Latin *philosophus* (philosopher) and -*aster* (a diminutive suffix with derogatory implication): a pretender or dabbler in philosophy.

> The evangelist asserted that anyone who claims to be a philosopher but who doubts God's existence is a mere **philosophaster**.

PHILTER (FIL-tur): *n.* from Greek *philos* (loving): love potion or charm.

> The psychologist said that there are no lucky charms or **philters** for making people fall in love.

PHILTRUM (FIL-trum): *n.* from Greek *philtron* (philter, charm, dimple in the upper lip): the vertical groove on the median line of the upper lip.

> Pete painted his **philtrum** with shoe polish, giving himself a Hitlerian moustache.

PHRONTISTERY (**FRAHN**-tis-TER-ee): *n.* from Greek *phrontistērion*, from *phrontistēs* (philosopher, deep thinker, person with intellectual pretensions): i. a place for thinking or study; ii. a school.

James referred to his study as "the **phrontistery**."

PILGARLIC (pil-GAHR-lik): *n.* from pilled garlic, meaning peeled garlic: i. a bald head; ii. a bald-headed man; iii. a man looked upon with humorous contempt or mock pity.

On *The Dick Van Dyke Show*, Buddy would often draw humorous attention to Mel's baldness, treating Mel as a **pilgarlic** in multiple senses of the term.

PILOSISM (PY-luh-siz'm): *n.* from Latin *pilosus* (hairy): excessive or abnormal hairiness.

Buford's **pilosism** was particularly noticeable when he was swimming with the almost hairless young boys.

piscation

PISCATION (puh-SKAY-shin): *n.* from Late Latin *piscatio*, from Late *piscatus*, past participle of *piscari* (to fish): fishing.

Although I enjoy eating fish, I'm not fond of **piscation**.

PISMIRISM (PIZ-mi-riz'm): *n.* from Middle English *pis-semire*, from *pisse* (piss) and *mire* (ant), of Scandinavian origin: the saving of every bit of money, such as hoarding pennies.

> Because Will was a wealthy man with a reputation for **pismirism**, we were not surprised to discover his closet filled with thousands of dollars in pennies.

PISTIC (PIS-tik): *adj.* from Late Latin *pisticus*, from Greek *pistikos*, from *pistis* (faith): of, relating to, or exhibiting faith.

> The televangelist asserted that all Christians, including political figures, must be free to express their **pistic** commitments.

PLATYOPIC (PLAT-ee-**AHP**-ik): *adj.* from Greek *plat-*, *platy-*, from *platys* (flat) and Greek *ōp-*, *ōps* (face, eye): having a broad flat face.

> Rarely will an actor with a nondescript, **platyopic** face become famous.

PLEONASM (**PLEE**-uh-NAZ-uhm): *n.* from Late Latin *pleonasmus*, from Greek *pleonasmas*, from *pleonazein* (to be more, to be in excess): i. the use of more words than are required to express an idea; ii. a redundancy.

> The expression "cease and desist" is a **pleonasm**.

PLEONEXIA (PLEE-uh-**NEK**-see-uh): *n.* from Greek *pleonektein* (to be greedy, to have or want more): greed, covetousness.

The economist asserted that we should not condemn capitalism because of the **pleonexia** of a few corporate leaders.

PLUTOLATRY (ploo-TAHL-uh-tree): *n.* from Greek-derived *plut-, ploutos* (wealth, riches) and *-latry, -latreia* (service, worship): excessive devotion to or worship of wealth.

The **plutolatry** of the corporate managers prompted them to lie about their company to manipulate the value of the stock.

POGONIASIS (POH-goh-**NY**-uh-sis): *n.* from Greek *pogon* (beard) and *-iasis* (a diseased condition): beard growth on a woman.

Although **pogoniasis** may be accepted in some circuses, bearded women will often not be treated well in many contexts.

POLYLOGIZE (puh-LIL-uh-jyz): *v.* from Greek *poly-, polys* (many, very) and *logos* (word, discourse): to talk excessively.

We must not **polylogize** about the problem; rather, we must act.

POLYMATH (**PAHL**-lee-MATH): *n.* from Greek *polymathēs* (knowing much), from *poly-* (many, very) and *-mathēs*, from *mathein, mathanein* (to learn): one of encyclopedic learning.

The author Isaac Asimov, a true **polymath**, wrote about 450 books, covering every category included in the library's Dewey Decimal System.

POLYPHAGE (PAHL-i-fayj): *n.* from Latin *polyphagus* (gourmand), from Greek *polyphagos* (eating too much): one eating much or many kinds of food.

Neil was a voracious **polyphage**, easy to please because he liked food of almost any sort.

POSTPRANDIAL (pohst-PRAN-dee-uhl): *adj.* from Latin *post* (after) and *prandium* (lunch): of, relating to, or occurring after a meal, especially dinner.

Because the dinner began late, the **postprandial** speeches had to be cut short.

PREMIATE (PREE-mee-AYT): *v.* from Medieval Latin *praemiatus*, past participle of *praemiare* (to reward): to give a prize or premium to or for.

premiate

The judge of the contest was honored to **premiate** the winner.

PRIDIAN (PRID-ee-uhn): *adj.* from Latin *pridianus*, from *pridie* (on the day before): of, or relating to a previous day or to yesterday.

We must deal with today and prepare for the future instead of having our minds absorbed by **pridian** events.

PROCACIOUS (proh-KAY-shuhs): *adj.* from Latin *procax* (impudent), from *procare* (to ask, demand): impudent.

The **procacious** adolescent liked burping at the dinner table.

PROPINATION (prah-puh-NAY-shin): *n.* from Latin *propinatio* (a drinking to someone's health, a toast): the act of drinking to someone's health.

We enjoyed the fine brandy we used in the **propination**, and Xander appreciated our wishing him well.

PROXENETE (**PRAHKS**-uh-NEET): *n.* from French *proxénète*, from Latin *proxeneta*, from Greek *proxenētēs*, from *proxenein* (to do something for someone else): marriage broker, matchmaker.

Modern people, who often use online dating services, would balk at choosing a marital partner through the services of a **proxenete**.

PSEUDODOX (**SOO**-duh-DAHKS): *n.* from Greek *pseudodoxos* (holding a false opinion), from *pseudodoxein* (to hold a false opinion): a false opinion or doctrine.

A person who believes a **pseudodox** presumably doesn't know that it is false.

PUDIBUND (**PYOO**-duh-BUND): *adj.* from Latin *pudibundus*, from *pudere* (to be ashamed): prudish.

The **pudibund** substitute teacher was shocked to see students kiss in the class.

PURSY (PUH-see, PUHR-see): *adj.* from Middle English *pursy*, from Anglo-French *pursif*, alteration of Middle French *polsif*, from *polser* (to push, beat, breathe with difficulty): short-winded, especially because of corpulence.

George was a **pursy** man who would easily become winded from climbing even one flight of stairs.

PYGALGIA (py-GAL-jee-uh): *n.* from Greek *pyge*, *pyx* (rump, buttocks) and *algos* (pain): pain in the buttocks.

Victor's **pygalgia** was due to his having sat on his wallet.

PYKNIC (PIK-nik): *adj.* from Greek *pyknos/puknos* (devise, thick, compact): having a short, stocky physique.

pyknic

Ivan Putski, the "Polish Power," was a professional wrestler in the 1970s known for his skill, strength, and **pyknic** body.

PYSMATIC (piz-MAT-ik): *adj.* from Greek *pysma* (question): always asking questions or inquiring.

Socrates was a **pysmatic** man whose questions embarrassed and enraged many people.

QUAESTUARY (KWES-choo-air-ee): *adj.* from Latin *quaestus* (way of making money, trade, gain, profit), from *quaestus*, past participle of *quaerere* (to seek, gain, ask): profit-seeking.

The billionaire H. Ross Perot assured the public that he was running for the American presidency for patriotic, not **quaestuary**, reasons.

quaestuary

QUATOPYGIA (KWAY/KWAH-tuh-**PIJ**-ee-uh): *n.* from Latin *quatio* (to shake) and Greek *pyge* (buttocks): the shaking of the buttocks in walking, a word especially applied to an erotic feminine walk.

When Thelma's walk resembled the **quatopygia** of a stripper, her boss chided her.

QUEAN (KWEEN): *n.* from Middle English *quene*, from Old English *cwene* (woman): a prostitute.

Many **queans** will not directly offer their services, but will instead ask men whether they would like dates.

QUERIMONIOUS (**KWAIR**-uh-MOH-nee-uhs): *adj.* from Medieval Latin *querimoniosus*, from Latin *querimonia* (complaint): complaining, querulous.

It was impossible for the hotel staff to please the **querimonious** guest.

QUIDNUNC (KWID-nuhngk): *n.* from Latin *quid nunc?* (what now?): one overcurious about petty and ephemeral things: newsmonger, busybody, gossip.

The scandal-saturated magazines appeal to **quidnuncs** who can never learn enough about other people's business.

QUODLIBET (KWAHD-li-bet): *n.* from Latin *quod libet* (what you will, as you please): i. a subtle or debatable point, especially a theological or scholastic question proposed for argument or disputation; ii. a scholastic or theological debate over a highly subtle point.

The student of the philosopher Alfred North Whitehead would often argue theological **quodlibets** that interest a vanishingly small number of human beings.

QUOMODO (**KWOH**-muh-DOH): *n.* from Latin for in what manner, how: means, manner.

Selling Jim's house gave him the **quomodo** to pay off his debts.

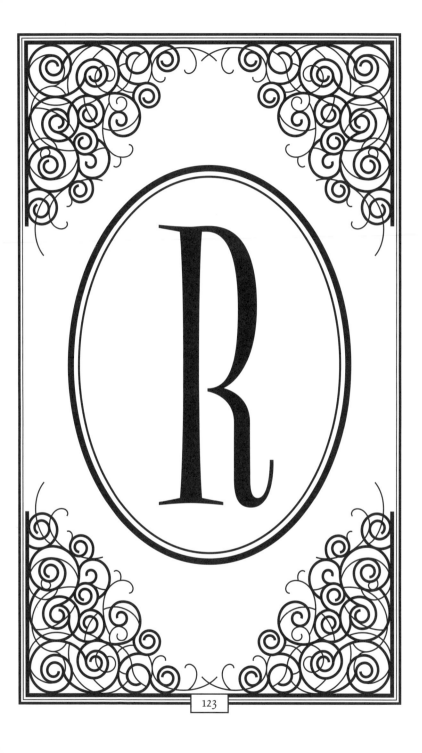

RANTIPOLE (RAN-ti-pohl): *n.* from *ranty* and *pole* (alteration of *poll*, head): a wild, unruly young person.

In the movie *The Wild One*, Marlon Brando played a motorcycle-riding **rantipole** who liked to break rules just for the fun of it.

RATAPLAN (rat-uh-PLAN): *n.* from French, an imitation of the sound: a repetitive beating or rapping sound, such as that of the rapid beating of a drum, the sound of galloping horses, or machine-gun fire.

In movies, there are devices for simulating the **rataplan** of galloping horses.

REBOATION (REB-oh-**AY**-shin): *n.* from Latin *reboatus*, past participle of *reboare* (to reverberate): a loud reverberation.

The **reboation** of a ship's horn can be heard for miles.

RECUMBENTIBUS (REK-um-**BEN**-ti-bus): *n.* from Latin *recumbent-*, *recumbens* (lying down) and *-ibus* (dative or ablative plural ending): a knockout punch (literally or figuratively).

Ronald Reagan executed a forensic **recumbentibus** when he turned the question whether he was too old to be president into a criticism of campaign opponent Walter Mondale's relative "inexperience."

RECUSANT (REK-yuh-zuhnt, ri-KYOO-zuhnt): *n.* from Latin *recusant-*, *recusans*, present participle of *recusare* (to object to, refuse): i. a Roman Catholic refusing to attend the services of the Church of England; ii. a nonconformist.

The rebellious adolescent delighted in being a **recusant**.

REPRISTINATE (REE-**PRIS**-tuh-NAYT): *v.* from *re-* (again) and *pristine*, from Latin *pristinus* (former, primitive, original): to restore to an original state or condition.

After Martha Stewart was released from prison, pundits disagreed over whether she would be able to **repristinate** her career.

RHATHYMIA (ruh-THY-mee-uh): *n.* from Greek *rhathymos* (light-hearted, easy-tempered, carefree): the state of being carefree: light-heartedness.

rhathymia

Beer commercials have traditionally presented people as delighting in festive **rhathymia**.

RHINOPHONIA (RY-nuh-**FOH**-nee-uh): *n.* from Greek-derived *rhino-*, *rhis*, *rhinos* (nose, snout) and *-phonia*, *phone* (sound, voice): extreme nasal sound in the voice.

Shelby was called Duckman because of his **rhinophonia**.

ROBORANT (ROB-uhr-uhnt): *adj.* from Latin *roborans*, *roborant-*, present participle of *roborare* (to strengthen): restoring vigor or strength.

Manny loved to take brisk walks for their **roborant** effects.

ROORBACK (ROOR-bak): *n.* from Baron Von *Roorback*, fictional author of *Roorback's Tour Through the Western and Southern States*, an imaginary book from which an alleged passage was quoted in the Ithaca (New York) *Chronicle* of 1844 that made scurrilous charges against James K. Polk, then Democratic candidate for the presidency: a defamatory falsehood published to harm someone politically, especially before an election.

> Political opponents of President George W. Bush published **roorbacks** reputing to document irregularities in his National Guard service.

RUBICUND (ROO-bi-KUHND): *adj.* from Latin *rubicundus* (red): ruddy.

> Daisy had a healthy **rubicund** complexion.

RUCTION (RUHK-shin): *n.* possibly from alteration of *insurrection*: a riotous disturbance or a noisy quarrel.

ruction

> Brandon felt uneasy when he heard the **ruction** of the two drunkards at the adjacent table.

RUDERAL (ROO-duhr-uhl): *adj.* from New Latin *ruderalis*, from Latin *rudus, ruder-* (rubbish): *of a plant*: growing in rubbish, poor land, or waste.

We were surprised to see the **ruderal** plant in the junkyard.

RUGOSE (ROO-gohs): *adj.* from Latin *rugosus* (wrinkled), from *ruga* (wrinkle): having many wrinkles or creases.

The elderly woman showed her age by her **rugose** cheeks.

RUPESTRIAN (roo-PES-tree-uhn): *adj.* from New Latin *rupestris* (rupestrian), from Latin *rupes* (rock): i. composed of rock; ii. inscribed on rocks.

On the cartoon show *The Flinstones*, newspapers and photographs were **rupestrian** instead of printed on paper.

SACCADE (sa-KAYD, sa-KAHD): *n.* from French, from Middle French, from *saquer, sachier* (to pull, draw): rapid movement of the eyes, especially the jerky motions one's eyes make as one looks quickly from one thing to another, as during reading.

> We could tell Cody was reading because of the **saccade** of his eyes.

SALTATION (SAL-**TAY**-sh<u>i</u>n): *n.* from Latin *saltation-, saltatio,* from *saltatus* (a dance): i. the action of leaping or jumping; ii. a dance or an act of dancing.

> Crickets are known for chirping and **saltation**.

SAPROPHAGOUS (s<u>a</u>-PRAHF-uh-g<u>u</u>s): *adj.* from Greek-derived *sapr-, sapros* (rotten) and *-phagus, phagein* (to eat): feeding on dead or decaying animal matter.

saprophagous

> While hiking, we saw the carcass of a rabbit covered with **saprophagous** insects.

SCHNORRER (SHNOR-ur): *n.* from Yiddish for beggar, from Middle High German *snurren* (to hum), from the sound of the musical instrument used by strolling beggars: a derogatory term for a person constantly mooching from others.

> Sam called his brother Sol a good-for-nothing **schnorrer** who would rather beg than work.

SCHOLASMS (SKOH-laz-<u>u</u>mz): *n.* from *scholastic*, on analogy with such pairs as English *enthusiastic/enthusiasm*: pedantic or academic expressions.

The professor was so accustomed to using **scholasms** that he often had trouble communicating with everyday people.

SCIALYTIC (SY-uh-lid/lit-ik): *adj.* from Greek *skia* (shade, shadow) and *lysis* (a losing, freeing, releasing): dispersing or dispelling shadows.

The **scialytic** device on the porch was a flood light.

SCIAMACHY (sy-AM-uh-kee): *n.* from Greek *skiamachia*, from *skia* (shadow) and *-machia, makhia* (fight): a fight with a shadow: a mock or futile combat (as with an imaginary opponent or foe).

Dennis was so belligerent that, if he could find no one to fight or argue with, he would engage in a **sciamachy**.

SCIOLIST (SY-uh-list): *n.* from Late Latin *sciolus* (smatterer), diminutive of Latin *scius* (knowing), from *scire* (to know): a person who pretends to be a scholar; an intellectual fake.

Craig was a **sciolist** who was entertaining at cocktail parties but whose pretension to scholarship was obvious to real experts.

SCOTOMA (skuh-TOH-muh): *n.* from Greek *skotōma*, from *skotoun* (to darken, blind), from *skotos* (darkness): a blind or dark spot in the visual field.

> When it came to acknowledging his son's immaturity, Gilbert had a **scotoma**.

SCRANNEL (SKRAN-uhl): *adj.* orgin unknown: grating on the ears: unmelodius.

> Leonard's background in classical music made it difficult for him to enjoy any music the least bit **scrannel**.

SIALOQUENT (sy-AL-uh-kwint): *adj.* from Greek *sialon* (saliva) and Latin *loqui* (to speak): spraying saliva while speaking.

> The **sialoquent** speaker's speech was so juicy that a heckler blurted, "Say it; don't spray it."

SIFFILATE (**SIF**-uh-LAYT): *v.* from modification of French *siffler* (to whistle): to whisper.

siffilate

> The librarian told us that if we felt impelled to communicate in the library we should either pass notes or **siffilate** our words.

SOMNILOQUIST (sahm-NIL-uh-kwist): *n.* from Latin *somnus* (sleep) and *loquor* (speak): one who talks in one's sleep.

The **somniloquist** unintentionally revealed his affair to his wife while he was asleep.

SOPHROSYNE (suh-FRAHS-uh-nee): *n.* from Greek *sōphrosynē*, from *sōphrōn* (being of sound mind, prudent, reasonable) and *-phron*, *phren* (mind): temperance or wise moderation.

Comedian John Belushi might be alive today had he practiced **sophrosyne** and not indulged in destructive behavior that led to a drug overdose.

SPADISH (SPAY-dish): *adj.* from *spade* (from the phrase *call a spade a spade*): direct and blunt in manner or expression.

The highly refined diplomat was taken aback by the **spadish** language used by the man next to him on the subway.

SPHETERIZE (**SFED**-uh-RYZ): *v.* from Greek *spheterizein*, from *spheteros* (their own, their): to take for one's own: appropriate.

If Rose doesn't make a will, there is a good chance that the government will **spheterize** a large portion of her assets after she dies.

SPIFLICATE (**SPIF**-luh-KAYT): *v.* origin unknown: i. to overcome or dispose of by violence; ii. to beat.

Garth was told that if he didn't want to be intimidated by the school bully, he'd need to **spiflicate** him and show his physical dominance.

STAGIARY (**STAY**-jee-ER-ee): *n.* from Medieval Latin *stagiarius*, from *stagium*, *estagium* (term of residence): a student of law.

Bill met Hillary as each was a **stagiary** at Yale Law School.

STEATOPYGIC (STEE-uh-tuh-**PIJ**-ik): *adj.* from Greek-derived *steat-*, *stear* (fat) and *pyge* (buttocks): having fat buttocks.

Women who don't want to go to the gym because they are **steatopygic** are like people who won't hire housemaids because they believe that their homes are too messy.

STELLIFORM (**STEL**-uh-FORM): *adj.* from New Latin *stelliformis*, from Latin *stella* (star): star-shaped.

stelliform

Nicki was disappointed that the planetarium wall decorations had stars painted as balls of light that weren't even vaguely **stelliform**.

STILLATITIOUS (**STIL**-uh-TISH-uhs): *adj.* from Latin *stillaticius*, from *stillatus*, past participle of *stillare* (to drip, trickle): falling in drops.

The **stillatitious** liquid we felt on our heads was rain.

STREPITOUS (STREP-uh-duhs): *adj.* from Latin *strepitus* (noise), from *strepere* (to make noise): noisy, boisterous, clamorous.

I couldn't hear Shirley because of the **strepitous** crowd.

SUBDOLOUS (SUHB-duh-luhs): *adj.* from Latin *sub* (under) and *dolus* (fraud, deceit): crafty, cunning, artful.

We were afraid to trust the **subdolous** car salesman, maybe because he was telling us what we wanted to hear.

SUBITANEOUS (suhb-uh-TAY-nee-uhs): *adj.* from Latin *subitaneus* (sudden): formed or taking place suddenly or unexpectedly.

The car accident was too **subitaneous** to have been prevented.

SUBREPTION (suh-BREP-shin): *n.* from Late Latin *subreption-*, *subreptio*, from Latin for act of stealing, from *subreptus*, past participle of *subripere* (to snatch away, take away secretly): a secret, underhanded, unlawful, or unfair representation through suppressing or fraudulently concealing facts.

The merchant's concealment of information important to evaluating the quality of his product bordered on **subreption**.

SUBRISIVE (sub-RYS/RYZ-iv): *adj.* from Latin *subrisus*, past participle of *subridere* (to smile): smiling.

We noticed Gillian's **subrisive** expressions during the joke.

subrisive

SUCCUS (SUHK-uhs): *n.* from Latin for *sucus* (juice): juice, especially expressed juice (as of a fruit) for medicinal use.

The man's health improved after he substituted water and **succus** for soft drinks.

SULLAGE (SUL-ij): *n.* probably from Middle French *souiller* (to soil): i. silt deposited by a current of waste; ii. waste materials or sewage; refuse.

Robert was upset when a sewer pipe burst, and his yard was filled with **sullage**.

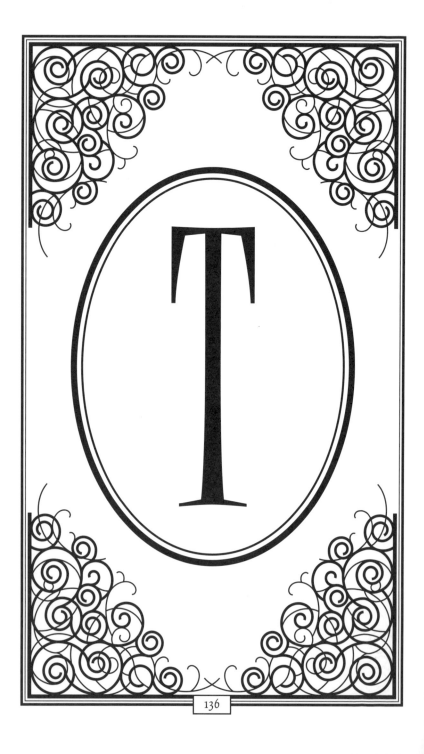

TANTIVY (TAN-ti-vee): *adv.* origin unknown: in a head-long dash, at a gallop.

The police officer ran **tantivy** after the robber.

TATTERDEMALION (TAT-ur-duh-**MAYL**-yu̱n): *n.* from *tatter* (a part torn and left hanging) and *-demalion* (origin unknown): i. a person dressed in ragged clothing; ii. one who is disreputable in appearance.

Because people usually judge others by their appearance, a **tatterdemalion** is often treated with less respect than that given to well-dressed persons.

TAUROMACHY (taw-RAHM-uh-kee): *n.* from Spanish *tauromaquia*, from Greek *tauromachia*, from *taurus* (bull) and *-machia* (fight): i. the art or practice of bullfighting; ii. bullfight.

The tourist didn't understand that in **tauromachy** the goal is to kill the bull.

TERATOLOGY (TER-uh-**TOL**-uh-jee): *n.* from Greek *teratologia*, from *teras* (monster): i. fantastic storytelling in which monsters play a large part; ii. the biological study of birth defects.

teratology

Fairy tales and epics that involve **teratology** really engage readers' imaginations.

TERMAGANT (TUR-muh-g<u>i</u>nt): *n.* from Middle English *Tervagant, Termagant* (imaginary Muslim deity represented in medieval mystery plays as a boisterous character): an overbearing, quarrelsome, scolding, or nagging woman: shrew, virago.

> The **termagant** would often lose her temper and beat her meek husband.

THALASSOCRACY (THAL-uh-**SAHK**-ruh-see): *n.* from Greek *thalassokratia*, from *thalassa* (sea) and *-kratia* (rule): maritime supremacy.

> For many years the British navy enjoyed their **thalassocracy**.

THAUMATURGE (THAW-muh-turj): *n.* from Greek *thaumatourgos* (working miracles), from *thauma* (miracle, wonder) and *ergon* (work): a performer of miracles.

> The rate of recovery of the doctor's patients was so extraordinary that he was regarded as a **thaumaturge**.

THELYTOKOUS (thuh-LID-**uh**-uh-k<u>u</u>s): *adj.* from *thēlytokos* (bearing females): producing only females.

> Laura and George W. Bush are **thelytokous** parents who are proud of their two daughters.

THRASONICAL (thruh-SAHN-uh-kuhl): *adj.* from Latin *Thraso* (Thraso), braggart soldier in the comedy *Eunuchus* by Roman playwright Terence: bragging, boastful.

The **thrasonical** man irritated people by his constant recitation of his accomplishments.

TINTAMARRE (tin-tuh-MAHR): *n.* from Middle French, from *tinter* (to ring), from Latin *tinnire* (to ring) and *-amarre* (origin unknown): a great confused noise: uproar, din.

Since Hank and Mildred were in a haunted house, they assumed that the **tintamarre** was produced by a poltergeist.

TINTINNABULAR (TIN-ti-**NAB**-yuh-luhr): *adj.* from Middle English, from Latin *tintinnabulum* (bell), from *tintinnare* (to jingle): of, or relating to bells or the ringing of bells.

tintinnabular

Because Donna's husband would always ring a bell when he wanted his wife to fetch him coffee, she called him "Mr. **Tintinnabular**."

TIQUEUR (ti-KUR): *n.* from French *tiqueur* (to have a tic, to twitch), from *tic* (tic): a person affected with a tic.

The comedian's deliberate facial contortions made him look like a **tiqueur**.

TITIVATE (**TID/TIT**-uh-VAYT): *v.* from *tidy* and *-vate* (as in *renovate*): to dress up (as by making small additions or alterations in attire): spruce up.

Mickey put on a tie to **titivate** his clothes for the meeting.

TONITRUOUS (toh-NI-troo-<u>us</u>): *adj.* from Latin *tonitruum* (thunder), from *tonitrus* (thunder): thundering, reverberating with the sound of thunder.

To cope with her fear of thunderstorms, Mrs. Davis would take a sedative as soon as she heard a **tonitruous** sound.

TRALATITIOUS (TRAL-uh-**TISH**-uhs): *adj.* from Latin *tralatitius*, from *tralatus*, *translatus*, suppletive past participle of *transferre* (to transfer): i. having a character, force, or significance transferred or derived from something extraneous: metaphorical, figurative; ii. passed along, as from hand to hand, mouth to mouth, or from generation to generation: handed down.

The story of *Jack and the Beanstalk* was a **tralatitious** tale circulating over time in several cultures.

TRANSPICUOUS (tranz-PIK-yuh-wuhs): *adj.* from New Latin *transpicuus*, from Latin *transpicere* (to look through, see through): clearly seen through or understood.

Roger's egoistic motives were **transpicuous**.

TRAULISM (TRAW-liz-uhm): *n.* from Greek *traulismos*, from *traulizein* (to mispronounce, lisp, stammer): stammering, stuttering.

Harry's usual glibness was replaced by **traulism** when he tried to speak to his date.

TREEN (TREE-uhn): *adj.* from Middle English, from Old English *trēowen*, from *trēow* (tree, wood): made of wood; wooden.

treen

The **treen** grandfather clock was made of oak.

TYRONIC (TY-rahn-ik): *adj.* from Latin *tiron-*, *tiro* (tyro): of, relating to, or characteristic of a tyro or beginner.

The **tyronic** essay was written by a student in a remedial English class.

UMBRATILE (**UHM**-bruh-TYL): *adj.* from Latin *umbratilis*, from *umbratus*, past participle of *umbrare* (to shade): carried on in seclusion.

The mugging was **umbratile**, so there were no witnesses.

URSIFORM (**UR**-suh-FORM): *adj.* from Latin *ursus* (bear): bear-shaped.

The campers were terrified when they saw an **ursiform** image outside their tent.

ursiform

UXORICIDE (uks-OR-i-syd): *n.* from Latin *uxor* (wife) and *-cide*, *caedo* (cut, kill): the murder of a wife by her husband.

Although wives sometimes kill their husbands, on *Court TV*, one is much more likely to see husbands who are accused of **uxoricide**.

VAGITUS (vuh-JY-t<u>u</u>s): *n*. from Latin *vagio* (to cry): the first cry of a newborn child.

> The **vagitus** of a newborn child is important to help the baby to breathe.

VALETUDINARIAN (VAL-uh-T(Y)OO-d<u>i</u>-**NAIR**-ee-in): *n*. from Latin *valetudinarius* (sickly, infirm), from *valetudin-*, *valetudo* (state of health, sickness), from *valere* (to be strong, be well): a weak or sickly person, especially one morbidly concerned with one's invalidism.

> The **valetudinarian** rarely talked about anything other than his illness and poor health.

VARLET (VAWR-lit): *n*. from Middle English, from Middle French *vallet*, *varlet*, *vaslet* (young nobleman, page, squire): a low, unprincipled person: rascal, knave.

varlet

> Although many Republicans disliked President Carter's policies, they never regarded him as a **varlet**.

VELITATION (VEL-uh-**TAY**-sh<u>i</u>n): *n*. from Latin *velitatus*, past participle of *velitari* (to skirmish): a minor dispute or slight contest: skirmish.

The general described his disagreement with some politicians in charge of military funding as a mere **velitation**, not a pitched battle.

VELLEITY (ve/vuh-LEE-i-tee): *n.* from New Latin *velleitas*, from Latin *velle* (to wish): a slight wish, without any desire to expend energy to fulfill it.

For many people, the desire to get into good physical condition is a mere **valleity** rather than a goal to which they are committed.

VENDITION (ven-DI-shin): *n.* from Latin *venditus*, past participle of *vendere* (to sell): the act of selling: sale.

Donald's grandfather was surprised to learn about the **vendition** of powdered urine from drug-free people to help users cheat on drug tests.

VENDUE (VEN-d(y)oo): *n.* from obsolete French, from Middle French, from *vendu*, past participle of *vendre* (to sell): a public sale at which goods are sold to the highest bidder: auction.

As the highest bidder, Roscoe left the **vendue** the owner of a classic Mustang.

VENENATE (VEN-uh-NAYT): *v.* from Latin *venenatus*, past participle of *venenare* (to poison): to poison.

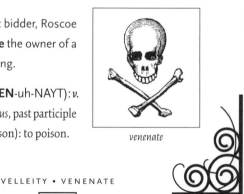

venenate

Gerald immediately called the veterinarian after he accidentally **venenated** the cat by bathing her in flea dip intended for dogs.

VENIREMAN (vuh-NY-ree-muhn): *n.* from Middle English *venire facias*, from Medieval Latin *venire* (facias), a phrase used from Latin ([you should cause] to come): a juror.

The **venireman** had trouble understanding the DNA expert who testified at the trial and so voted to acquit.

VERBIGERATE (vur-BIJ-ur-ayt): *v.* from Latin *verbigeratus*, past participle of *verbigerare* (to talk): to repeat a word or sentence endlessly, meaninglessly, and usually unconsciously.

The disoriented mental patient would rarely complete a sentence, but instead repeated certain phrases, **verbigerating** for hours.

VERIDICAL (vuh-RID-i-kuhl): *adj.* from Latin *veridicus* (veracious), from *verus* (true) and *dicere* (to say): i. truthful, veracious; ii. not illusory: genuine, real, actual.

The mathematician, scientist, and philosopher Descartes believed that we must use reason to distinguish **veridical** from illusory, sensory experience.

VERJUICE (VUR-joos): *n.* from Middle English *verjuis*, *verjus*, from Middle French *verjus* (green juice): i. the acidic juice of crab apples or other sour fruit, such as unripe grapes; ii. sourness, as of disposition.

Anthony's **verjuice** didn't make him many friends among his co-workers.

VERMIFORM (**VUR**-mi-FORM): *adj.* from *vermis* (worm) and -*formis* (form): wormlike.

Spaghetti noodles are **vermiform** in appearance.

VERRUCA (vuh-ROO-kuh): *n.* from Latin *verruca* (wart): a wart.

Because Theresa had a prominent **verruca** on her nose, other students would sometimes call her "the witch."

VESICATE (**VES**-i-KAYT): *v.* from New Latin *vesicare*, from *vesica* (bladder, blister): to blister or become blistered.

The mustard gas had **vesicated** the soldier's skin.

VESPINE (VES-pyn, VES-pin): *adj.* from Latin *vespa* (wasp): of, relating to, characteristic of, or resembling wasps.

Debbie was annoyed by Laura's **vespine** movements as she raced around the room to examine how well it was cleaned.

VIATICUM (vy-AT-i-kum): *n.* from Late Latin *viaticum*, from Latin, traveling provisions, from neuter of *viaticus*, from *via* (road): traveling supplies, possibly including transportation or money.

The businessman's **viaticum** enabled him to stay at a good hotel.

VIATOR (vy-AY-tuhr): *n.* from Latin *viator* (traveler): traveler.

The **viator** went alone on his trip.

VIBRISSAE (vy-BRIS-ee): *n.* from Latin *vibrissae* (hairs in the nostrils), probably from *vibrare* (to shake, vibrate): the whiskers of a cat.

A cat's **vibrissae** help it to achieve balance and determine whether it can fit through some narrow pathway.

VIDUITY (vi-DYOO-uh-tee): *n.* from Middle English (Scots) *viduite*, from Middle French *viduité*, from Latin *vidua* (widow): widowhood.

It is doubtful that, when Jacqueline Bouvier married John F. Kennedy, she ever expected to experience **viduity** at an early age.

VILLATIC (vi-LAD/LAT-ik): *adj.* from Latin *villaticus*, from *villa* (country house, country estate, village): of, or relating to a villa or a village: rural.

When Pamela would find the city too stressful, she'd go to her **villatic** cabin.

VINACEOUS (vy-NAY-shuhs): *adj.* from Latin *vinaceus* (of wine), from *vinum* (wine): i. having the color of red wine; ii. pertaining to wine.

The **vinaceous** draperies accented the gold hues in the room and pulled out the deep reds in the wallpaper.

VITELLUS (vi/vy-TEL-uhs): *n.* from Latin for little calf: the yolk of an egg.

Betsy would eat an egg white, but would avoid any **vitellus** because she was watching her intake of fats and cholesterol.

VIVISEPULTURE (**VIV**-uh-se-PUL-chur): *n.* from Latin *vividus* (animated) and *sepulcrum* (grave, tomb): the act or practice of burying alive.

Edgar Allan Poe wrote many horror stories playing on his fear of suffering **vivisepulture**, so it is ironic that many believe it was possible that he actually was buried alive.

VOLITANT (VAWL-i-tint): *adj.* from Latin *volitans, volitant-,* present participle of *volitare* (to fly to and fro): i. flying or capable of flying; ii. moving about rapidly.

volitant

A flying squirrel is not truly **volitant**, since it glides and doesn't fly.

VULGUS (VUHL-guhs): *n.* from Latin *vulgus* (the people, the public, the multitude): the common people.

Many people who have grown up in rich homes are out of touch with the financial problems encountered by the **vulgus**.

WAMBLE (WAHM/WAM-b<u>ul</u>): *n./v.* from Middle English *wamlen* (to feel nausea): i. *n.* the rumble, gurgle, or growl made by a distressed stomach; ii. an upset stomach; iii. *v.* to rumble or growl (as in a stomach).

> After Horace had eaten three hot dogs, three tacos, and boiled cabbage, he felt ill and his stomach began to **wamble**.

WELTANSCHAUUNG (VEL-tahn-showng): *n.* from German *Welt* (world) and *Anschauung* (view): worldview, that is, a comprehensive philosophy or view of life.

weltanschauung

> The atheistic scientist asserted that his **Weltanschauung** does not include the supernatural.

WHIFFLER (HWIF/WIF-luhr): *n.* from obsolete English *wifle* (battle-ax), from Middle English, from Old English *wifel* (dart, javelin): one who clears the way for a procession.

> Because Sean loved attention, he was the ideal **whiffler** to lead the parade.

WHIGMALEERIE (**HWIG**-muh-LEE-ree): *n.* origin unknown: i. whim, vagary, fancy; ii. an odd, fanciful contrivance.

The eccentric old man was full of caprice and **whig-maleeries**.

WIDDERSHINS (**WID**-uhr-SHINZ): *adv.* from Middle Low German *weddersinnes,* from Middle High German *widersinnes,* from *widersinnen* (to go back, go against): in a left-handed or contrary direction: contrarily, counterclockwise.

Clara immediately turned to the right because she believed that it is unlucky to walk in a church **widdershins**.

WITTOL (WIT′l): *n.* from Middle English *wetewold,* from *weten, witen* (to be aware, know) and *-wold* (as in cokewold, cuckold): i. a man who meekly or tacitly accepts his wife's adultery; a cuckold; ii. a half-witted person.

Some **wittols** accept the infidelity of their wealthy wives because of economic benefits.

WOWSER (WOW-zur): *n.* origin unknown: an obtrusively puritanical person censoriously hostile to minor vices and various forms of popular amusements.

Members of Afghanistan's Taliban government were, so to speak, **wowsers** on steroids, banning even kite-flying as an unacceptable distraction from righteousness.

XANTHIC (ZAN-thik): *adj.* from Greek *xanthos* (yellow): of, relating to, or tending toward yellow.

Because Nancy loved yellow, she would often grow **xanthic** flowers.

XANTHIPPE (zan-TIP-ee): *n.* from *Xanthippe*, wife of Socrates: an ill-tempered woman: shrew.

Sometimese insecure men will unfairly refer to an assertive woman as a **Xanthippe**.

XENODOCHEIONOLOGY (ZEN-uh-duh-KY-uh-**NAHL**-uh-jee): *n.* from Greek *xenodocheion* (inn): the lore of hotels and inns.

The author had visited dozens of hotels before writing his book on **xenodocheionology**.

XERIC (ZER-ik): *adj.* from Greek *xēros* (dry): of, characterized by, or adapted to an extremely dry habitat.

Nick's dislike of humidity caused him to settle in **xeric** Phoenix, Arizona.

XIPHOID (ZY-foyd): *adj.* from New Latin *xiphoides*, from Greek *xiphoeidēs*, from *xiphos* (sword): shaped like a sword.

xiphoid

Even though Benny's sword was a plastic toy, he was required to leave it in his car because its **xiphoid** appearance raised suspicions.

XYLOID (ZY-loyd): *adj.* from Greek *xylon* (wood): resembling wood: woody.

The tree was not wood at all but fiberglass painted to appear **xyloid**.

YENTA (YEN-tuh): *n.*
from Yiddish *yenta* (vulgar
or sentimental woman),
from the name *Yente*: one
who meddles or gossips.

yenta

Izzy knew that if he
told one **yenta**, every-
one in the synagogue would know the secret.

YESTREEN (ye-STREEN): *n.* from Middle English
(Scots) *yistrevin*, from *yisterday* (yesterday) and *evin* (evening):
yesterday evening.

Wanda started to prepare the turkey **yestreen** so that
the cooking would be done in time today for the
Thanksgiving feast.

ZAFTIG (ZAHF-tig): *adj.* from Yiddish *zaftik* (juicy, succulent), from *zaft* (juice, sap), from Middle High German *saf*, *saft*, from Old High German *saf*: having a full, rounded figure: pleasingly plump.

zaftig

Although Marilyn Monroe was considered tantalizingly **zaftig** in her time, she would be considered overweight by today's standards for models and actresses.

ZETETIC (zuh-TET-ik): *adj.* from Greek *zētētikos*, from *zētētos*, verbal of *zētein* (to seek for, inquire): proceeding by inquiry.

Socrates was famous for his **zetetic** conversations, in which he would question people about the nature of piety, knowledge, and wisdom.

ZOETIC (ZOH-ed/et-ik): *adj.* from Greek *zōē* (life): of, or relating to life: living, vital.

We enjoyed the **zoetic** interaction of the petting zoo.

ZOONOSIS (zoh-AHN-uh-sis, ZOH-uh-**NOH**-sis): *n.* from Greek *zōo-*, *zōio-*, from *zōion* (living being) and Greek *nosos* (disease): a disease of animals, such as rabies, that can be transmitted to human beings.

Tommy's rabies was a **zoonosis** contracted when he was bitten by a raccoon.

THE REVERSE
DICTIONARY

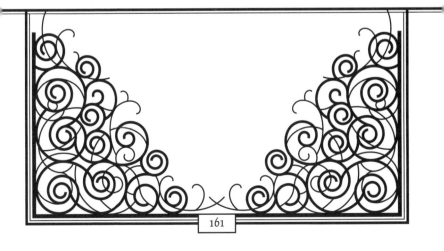

A NOTE ABOUT THE REVERSE DICTIONARY

Although the main part of this book is organized as a conventional dictionary, this appendix is a reverse dictionary, in which definitions of terms are listed alphabetically. Such an arrangement is particularly useful when the definition of a term is much more familiar to most people than the term itself. Accordingly, while people are familiar with the concept of the murder of a wife by her husband, they may be unfamiliar with the word "uxoricide." This reverse dictionary will enable the reader to discover the word "uxoricide" by going to different formulations of the same underlying concept. Consequently, the reader can find the word "uxoricide" next to either the definition "murder of a wife by her husband" or the definition "wife, murder of one's." By providing readers with more than one formulation of an underlying concept, the reverse dictionary enhances the chances that they will find and remember the "gilded" term for that concept. Not every term is given multiple definitions, but many terms are, especially when multiple definitions are useful.

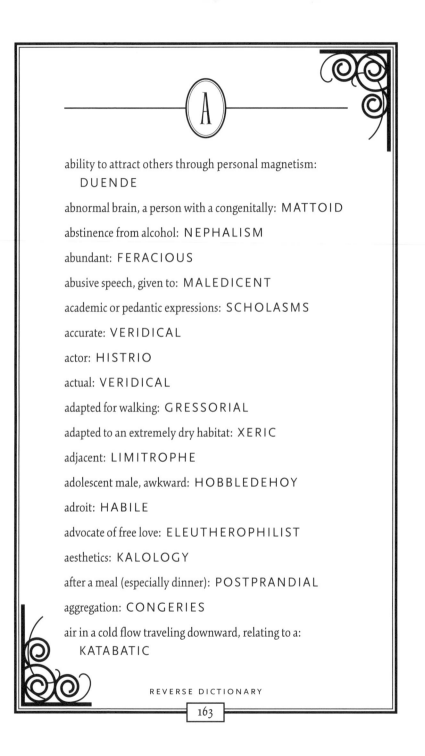

A

ability to attract others through personal magnetism:
  DUENDE

abnormal brain, a person with a congenitally: MATTOID

abstinence from alcohol: NEPHALISM

abundant: FERACIOUS

abusive speech, given to: MALEDICENT

academic or pedantic expressions: SCHOLASMS

accurate: VERIDICAL

actor: HISTRIO

actual: VERIDICAL

adapted for walking: GRESSORIAL

adapted to an extremely dry habitat: XERIC

adjacent: LIMITROPHE

adolescent male, awkward: HOBBLEDEHOY

adroit: HABILE

advocate of free love: ELEUTHEROPHILIST

aesthetics: KALOLOGY

after a meal (especially dinner): POSTPRANDIAL

aggregation: CONGERIES

air in a cold flow traveling downward, relating to a:
  KATABATIC

alcoholic beverages, total abstinence from: NEPHALISM

alcoholism: DIPSOMANIA

all kinds: OMNIFARIOUS

all-nighter, pulling a: PERNOCTATION

anguish, something relieving: DOLORIFUGE

animal copulation, abnormal desire to watch:
FAUNOIPHILIA

animal disease capable of being transmitted to people
(such as rabies): ZOONOSIS

apathy, spiritual: ACEDIA

aphorism: APOTHEGM

argument, contest, or skirmish, a minor: VELITATION

arrogant demeanor: HAUTEUR

assertion, unsupported and dogmatic: IPSEDIXITISM

attraction to a male younger than oneself: KOROPHILIA

auction: VENDUE

award a prize: PREMIATE

B

babbling, foolish person: BLATHERSKITE

back pain: DORSODYNIA

bad breath: OZOSTOMIA

bad habit: CACOËTHES

bad taste, in: LOUCHE

bald: GLABROUS

bald-headed man, hapless: PILGARLIC

bark: LATRATE

base coward: CAITIFF

bawdy (especially in lyrics or verse): FESCENNINE

beard growth, female: POGONIASIS

bear-shaped: URSIFORM

beat, violently: SPIFLICATE

beat with a club: FUSTIGATE

beauty, overestimation of: KALOPSIA

beauty, study of: KALOLOGY

beer foam: BARM

beggar licensed in Scotland to accept alms: GABERLUNZIE

beginners, relating to: TYRONIC

behind the scenes, side: COULISSE

belief that the human race descended from two persons,
    such as Adam and Eve: MONOGENISM

bells, relating to: TINTINNABULAR

bending or winding: FLEXUOUS

best: PALMARY

best, being the: OPTIMITY

Bible-seller, itinerant: COLPORTEUR

big-bellied: ABDOMINOUS

birth defects, study of: TERATOLOGY

birth, giving: PARTURITION

birth to a god, giving: DEIPAROUS

biting one's nails: ONYCHOPHAGY

black, purplish: MURREY

blend: INOSCULATE

blindness, night: NYCTALOPIA

blind spot: SCOTOMA

blister: VESICATE

blockhead: MOME

blunt: SPADISH

boastful: THRASONICAL

boastful and self-important man: COCKALORUM

boastful display or declaration: JACTATION

boastfulness: GASCONADE

body hair, bristling of: HORRIPILATION

body that is long and slender, one having a: LEPTOSOME

bombastic or pompous language: GRANDILOQUENCE

books, a dealer in used or rare: BIBLIOPOLE

bookseller (especially of the Bible): COLPORTEUR

bookworm: BIBLIOPHAGE

bottomless pit: BARATHRUM

boy, gawky: HOBBLEDEHOY

bragging: THRASONICAL

brain, a person with a congenitally abnormal: MATTOID

bravado: GASCONADE

breakable: FRANGIBLE

breast cleavage, having deep: BATHYCOLPIAN

breath, bad: OZOSTOMIA

breathing strenuously or being short-winded: PURSY

brick-red: LATERITIOUS

bright: NITID

brittle: FRANGIBLE

broad flat face, having a: PLATYOPIC

brothel: BAGNIO, LUPANAR

build a nest: NIDIFICATE

bullfight: TAUROMACHY

burning meat, the smell of: NIDOR

burying alive, the act of: VIVISEPULTURE

bushy: BOSKY

busybody: QUIDNUNC

butter, resembling: BUTYRACEOUS

buttocks: NATES

buttocks, having beautiful: CALLIPYGIAN

buttocks, having fat: STEATOPYGIC

buttocks, pain in the: PYGALGIA

buttocks, shaking of the: QUATOPYGIA

buy, an uncontrollable itch to: EMACITY, ONIOMANIA

C

calculated to confuse, entrap, or entangle: CAPTIOUS

cannibal: ANTHROPOPHAGUS

car, lovemaking in a: AMOMAXIA

carefree, state of being: RHATHYMIA

cathartic: LAPACTIC

cat, old and female: GRIMALKIN

cat whiskers: VIBRISSAE

champagne wire cage: AGRAFFE

chance, depending on: ALEATORY

charisma: DUENDE

cheap and gaudy: BRUMMAGEM

cheerful: EUPEPTIC

chew food at least thirty times: FLETCHERIZE

childbirth: PARTURITION

childless woman: NULLIPARA

children, production of many: PHILOPROGENEITY

chin: MENTUM

civil order under good laws: EUNOMY

clear in thought or expression: LUCULENT

cleavage, having deep: BATHYCOLPIAN

cleverly creative or resourceful: DAEDALIAN

coin-shaped: NUMMIFORM

cold flow of air traveling downward, relating to a:
    KATABATIC

cold, icy: GELID

collection: CONGERIES

colonizer: OECIST

color of bricks: LATERITIOUS

color of red wine: VINACEOUS

commendation, worthy of: PALMARY

common people: VULGUS

complaining: QUERIMONIOUS

composed of both good and evil:
    AGATHOKAKOLOGICAL

compulsion: COACTION

concealing, act of: OBVELATION

concealment of facts: SUBREPTION

conceited or impudent person: JACKANAPES

concern for others: ALTEROCENTRIC

condescending demeanor: HAUTEUR

confuse, calculated to: CAPTIOUS

congratulate: FELICITATE

connoisseur of wine: OENOPHILIST

constipated: COSTIVE

constructed, badly: INCONDITE

contest or argument, a minor: VELITATION

continuous, to make: INOSCULATE

contrarily: WIDDERSHINS

corridor, side: COULISSE

corruption in a position: MALVERSATION

cosmetics, to apply: FARD

cough syrup: LINCTUS

counterclockwise: WIDDERSHINS

covetousness: PLEONEXIA

coward: CAITIFF

crackling sound: CREPITATION

crafty: SUBDOLOUS

crescent-shaped body part: LUNULA

criticize harshly: FUSTIGATE

cross-bearing: CRUCIFEROUS

crossword puzzle creator or expert: CRUCIVERBALIST

crown with or as if with a laurel: LAUREATE

crude and sloppy person: GROBIAN

crying out together: CONCLAMANT

cuckold: WITTOL

cult of the obscene: AISCHROLATREIA

culturally backward and stupid: BOEOTIAN

cunning: SUBDOLOUS

cure-all: CATHOLICON

curse: MALISON

dance: SALTATION

danger or risk, expose to: PERICLITATE

dead or decaying animal matter, feeding on:
    SAPROPHAGOUS

decorative metal plate around keyhole or doorknob:
    ESCUTCHEON

defamatory falsehood published to harm someone: ROORBACK

defecating, difficulty in: DYSCHEZIA

defecating, pain in: DYSCHEZIA

deflowering a virgin: HYMENORRHEXIS

delusion that things are more beautiful than they are: KALOPSIA

derived from something extraneous (as in something metaphorical or figurative): TRALATITIOUS

desire to buy things, uncontrollable: EMACITY, ONIOMANIA

desire, uncontrollable: CACOËTHES

desk, writing: ESCRITOIRE

dinner conversation, skillful: DEIPNOSOPHY

direct and blunt in speech: SPADISH

discharge from an inflamed bodily orifice: GLEET

disease of animals capable of being transmitted to people: ZOONOSIS

dishonesty: IMPROBITY

disordered assemblage (as of words): FARRAGO

dispelling sleep: HYPNOPOMPIC

dispute, minor: VELITATION

doctrine emphasizing faith over reason: FIDEISM

dogmatic assertion: IPSEDIXITISM

dog, to bark like a: LATRATE

doleful: FLEBILE

downy: LANUGINOUS

dream interpreter: ONEIROCRITIC

dress up (as by making small additions): TITIVATE

drinking, fond of: BIBULOUS

drinking to someone's health: PROPINATION

drops, falling in: STILLATITIOUS

drug or potion removing sad memories: NEPENTHE

drum roll: PARADIDDLE

dry habitat, adapted to a: XERIC

duel: MONOMACHY

dull and tedious passage or section (as of a work or a play):
    LONGUEUR

dullness in mind or body: HEBETUDE

dung-eating: COPROPHAGOUS, MERDIVOROUS

E

ears, having large: MACROTOUS

eater of much or many kinds of food: POLYPHAGE

eating dung: COPROPHAGOUS, MERDIVOROUS

eating frogs: BATRACHOPHAGOUS

eating grass: GRAMINIVOROUS

eating, one who refrains from: JEJUNATOR

eating together, the practice of: COMMENSALITY

economic self-sufficiency: AUTARKY

edible: COMESTIBLE

egg yolk: VITELLUS

elbow, bony tip of: OLECRANON

elderly female cat: GRIMALKIN

eloquence: FACUNDITY

embezzlement: DEFALCATION

eminent person: EMINENTO

encyclopedic knowledge, person with: POLYMATH

encyclopedic reading, characterized by: OMNILEGENT

enjoyment of foolish trifles: DESIPIENCE

enormous: BROBDINGNAGIAN

esoteric: ACROAMATIC

examination of an object by the unaided eye:
    MACROGRAPHY

examination, to supervise an: INVIGILATE

examine thoroughly: PERLUSTRATE

excellent: EXIMIOUS

excess: NIMIETY

excessive use of "he" in reference to oneself: ILLEISM

excrement-eating: MERDIVOROUS

execute by stoning: LAPIDATE

experimental: PEIRASTIC

explosion, loud and violent: FULMINATION

expressing feelings rather than stating facts: PHATIC

extreme (especially in a derogatory sense): ARRANT

eyebrows, flat area between: GLABELLA

eyelids, located on or near the: PALPEBRAL

eye movement, rapid and jerky: SACCADE

eye soreness: LIPPITUDE

face, having one that is broad and flat: PLATYOPIC

faint, tending to: LIPOTHYMIC

faith, doctrine stressing the need for: FIDEISM

faith, expressing: PISTIC

faith, strict adherence to one's: ORTHOPRAXY

faith, tepid in one's: LAODICEAN

fake intellectual: SCIOLIST

falling in drops: STILLATITIOUS

false memory: PARAMNESIA

false opinion: PSEUDODOX

family name: COGNOMEN

farm horse, working: DOBBIN

fasts, one who: JEJUNATOR

fat buttocks, having: STEATOPYGIC

faultfinding: CAPTIOUS

faulty act (as a slip of tongue or memory): PARAPRAXIS

fearless: IMPAVID

feeblemindedness: OLIGOPHRENIA

feeding on dead or decaying animal matter:
    SAPROPHAGOUS

fighting with a shadow: SCIAMACHY

figurative: TRALATITIOUS

figure, having a full and rounded: ZAFTIG

filth that is sticky, slimy, or greasy and from a bodily
    orifice: GLEET

filth, the worship of: AISCHROLATREIA

filthy: IMMUND

filthy or obscene literature, study of: COPROLOGY

finger, little: MINIMUS

fingernail, half-moon pale area at the base of: LUNULA

finicky: NIMINY-PIMINY

first cry of a newborn child: VAGITUS

fishing: PISCATION

flat area of forehead between eyebrows: GLABELLA

flat face, having a: PLATYOPIC

flatterer, servile: LICKSPITTLE

flesh, the creeping of: HORRIPILATION

fleshy bulbs on each side of the nose: ALAE

flourish added to one's signature: PARAPH

flying, capable of: VOLITANT

foam on beer: BARM

focusing attention and concern on others:
    ALTEROCENTRIC

fond of drinking: BIBULOUS

food, plundering of: CLEPTOBIOSIS

fool: MOME

foolish act: BÊTISE

foolish trifles, relaxed enjoyment of: DESIPIENCE

forbearance: LONGANIMITY

forehead, flat area between eyebrows: GLABELLA

forgetting, act of: OBLIVESCENCE

formed or occurring suddenly or unexpectedly:
SUBITANEOUS

found in both northern and southern hemispheres:
AMPHIGEAN

fragile: FRANGIBLE

freckled, extremely: LENTIGINOUS

free love, advocate of: ELEUTHEROPHILIST

frenzied: FURIBUND

frog-eating: BATRACHOPHAGOUS

fruitful: FERACIOUS

full and rounded figure, having a: ZAFTIG

functional, practical, or utilitarian: BANAUSIC

funds, embezzling or misappropriating: DEFALCATION

fur, covered with soft: LANUGINOUS

gallop, at a: TANTIVY

gap between adjacent teeth: EMBRASURE

gawky adolescent boy: HOBBLEDEHOY

gentleness, mildness, or meekness: MANSUETUDE

genuine: VERIDICAL

giving birth: PARTURITION

giving birth to a god: DEIPAROUS

glass, resembling: HYALINE

glossy: NITID

gods, the worship of foreign or unsanctioned: ALLOTHEISM

good digestion, having: EUPEPTIC

good laws, a system of: EUNOMY

goods thrown overboard with a buoy attached: LAGAN

goose bumps: HORRIPILATION

gooselike: ANSERINE

gossiper: QUIDNUNC, YENTA

government by mob rule: OCHLOCRACY

government by the worst people: KAKISTOCRACY

government by women: GYNARCHY

grass-eating: GRAMINIVOROUS

grating sound, having a: SCRANNEL

great confused noise: TINTAMARRE

greed: PLEONEXIA

greedy: LICKERISH

gregarious: AMADELPHOUS

grief, something that dispels: DOLORIFUGE

grinding one's teeth, act of: BRUXOMANIA

ground, to lie on the: HUMICUBATE

growing in rubbish, poor land, or waste: RUDERAL

growing or formed in lakes: LACUSTRINE

growling in the stomach: BORBORYGMUS

gullible person: GOBEMOUCHE

hair, having straight: LEIOTRICHOUS

hairiness, excessive: PILOSISM

hair, without: GLABROUS

half, a: MOIETY

half-moon pale area at the base of the fingernail or toenail: LUNULA

half-witted person: WITTOL

handed down from generation to generation:
TRALATITIOUS

handwriting, abnormally large: MACROGRAPHY

handwriting flourish made at the end of a signature:
PARAPH

handwriting, sloppy or illegible: GRIFFONAGE

happiness, inability to experience: ANHEDONIA

hatred of marriage: MISOGAMY

hatred of what is new or changed, characterized by:
MISONEISTIC

headlong dash, in a: TANTIVY

hedonist: FRANION

"he," excessive use of: ILLEISM

Hell: BARATHRUM

hemispheres, found in both: AMPHIGEAN

hickeys, the practice of producing: DERMAGRAPHISM

hoarding money: PISMIRISM

hold (as a lion) at bay: DOMPT

holiday, going on: FERIATION

horse, working farm: DOBBIN

hotel-lore: XENODOCHEIONOLOGY

human descent from two persons, belief in:
MONOGENISM

hunger, extraordinary: EDACITY

I

icy, cold: GELID

idler: FAINÉANT

illegible or bad handwriting: G R I F F O N A G E

illiterate person: A N A L P H A B E T

ill-tempered woman: T E R M A G A N T, X A N T H I P P E

immense: B R O B D I N G N A G I A N

immortality-conferring Hindu beverage: A M R I T A

imperil: P E R I C L I T A T E

impudent: P R O C A C I O U S

impudent or conceited person: J A C K A N A P E S

inability to experience pleasure or happiness: A N H E D O N I A

inability to recall the proper meanings of words:
    P A R A M N E S I A

indifferent in religious or political conviction: L A O D I C E A N

indisputable: I R R E F R A G A B L E

individual, peculiar to an: I D I O P A T H I C

industrious: O P E R O S E

ineffectual or useless: F R U S T R A N E O U S

inflammation of a bodily orifice: G L E E T

influence of past on present: M O R T M A I N

inquiring constantly: P Y S M A T I C

inquiry, proceeding by: Z E T E T I C

insane, a person who is partly: M A T T O I D

inscribed in rock: R U P E S T R I A N

integrity, lack of: IMPROBITY

intellectual fake: SCIOLIST

intellectuals, literati, or scholars collectively: CLERISY

intelligentsia: CLERISY

intermediate: MESOTHETIC

interpreter of dreams: ONEIROCRITIC

interrogatory or questioning: PYSMATIC

intestinal gas, rumbling sound of: BORBORYGMUS

introduction to a scholarly subject: ISAGOGE

inventive, extraordinarily: DAEDALIAN

irresponsible idler: FAINÉANT

jerk about: JACTITATE

judgment, habitually suspending: EPHECTIC

juice (especially when used as medicine): SUCCUS

juice, sour: VERJUICE

jumping or leaping: SALTATION

juror: VENIREMAN

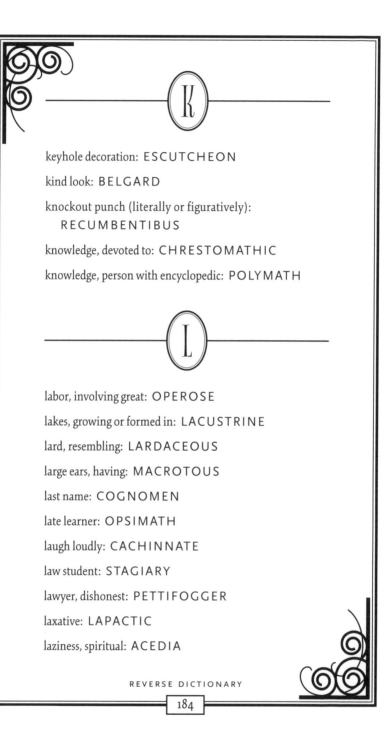

K

keyhole decoration: ESCUTCHEON

kind look: BELGARD

knockout punch (literally or figuratively):
RECUMBENTIBUS

knowledge, devoted to: CHRESTOMATHIC

knowledge, person with encyclopedic: POLYMATH

L

labor, involving great: OPEROSE

lakes, growing or formed in: LACUSTRINE

lard, resembling: LARDACEOUS

large ears, having: MACROTOUS

last name: COGNOMEN

late learner: OPSIMATH

laugh loudly: CACHINNATE

law student: STAGIARY

lawyer, dishonest: PETTIFOGGER

laxative: LAPACTIC

laziness, spiritual: ACEDIA

leaping or jumping: SALTATION

learned people collectively: CLERISY

learner, a late: OPSIMATH

learning, relating to: PALLADIAN

lecherous: LICKERISH

leech, relating to a: HIRUDINOID

legal specialist: LEGIST

lethargy: HEBETUDE

liar, habitual: MYTHOMANE

lie prone or prostrate: HUMICUBATE

life, pertaining to: ZOETIC

light-heartedness: RHATHYMIA

lighthouse: PHAROS

limping: CLAUDICATION

linguistic expressions, given to using pretentious:
   LEXIPHANICISM

lips, having thick: LABROSE

lip, vertical groove on upper: PHILTRUM

literati, the: CLERISY

literature, filthy or obscene, study of: COPROLOGY

little finger or toe: MINIMUS

little man who thinks he's big: COCKALORUM

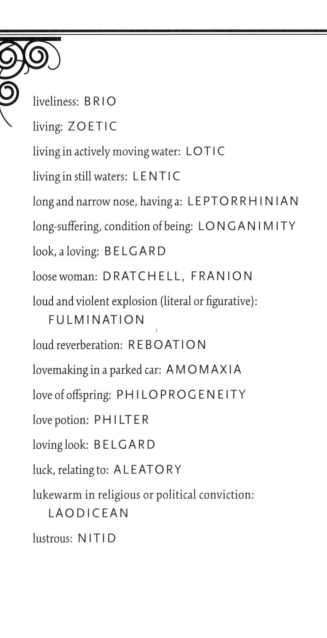

liveliness: B R I O

living: Z O E T I C

living in actively moving water: L O T I C

living in still waters: L E N T I C

long and narrow nose, having a: L E P T O R R H I N I A N

long-suffering, condition of being: L O N G A N I M I T Y

look, a loving: B E L G A R D

loose woman: D R A T C H E L L, F R A N I O N

loud and violent explosion (literal or figurative):
   F U L M I N A T I O N

loud reverberation: R E B O A T I O N

lovemaking in a parked car: A M O M A X I A

love of offspring: P H I L O P R O G E N E I T Y

love potion: P H I L T E R

loving look: B E L G A R D

luck, relating to: A L E A T O R Y

lukewarm in religious or political conviction:
   L A O D I C E A N

lustrous: N I T I D

make-up, paint face with: FARD

male political and social supremacy: ANDROCRACY

male younger than oneself, attraction to a: KOROPHILIA

mania: CACOËTHES

mania for holding public office: EMPLEOMANIA

manifestation: OSTENT

man who meekly or tacitly accepts his wife's adultery:
WITTOL

marital unhappiness: CAGAMOSIS

maritime supremacy: THALASSOCRACY

marriage at or above one's social station: HYPERGAMY

marriage formed only because of physical attraction:
GENECLEXIS

marriage, hatred of: MISOGAMY

marriage late in life: OPSIGAMY

marriage outside one's group: EXOGAMY

marriage, relating to: HYMENEAL

marriage with mismatched partners: HETEROGAMOSIS

mastery of all subjects, marked by: PANCRATIC

matchmaker: PROXENETE

means or manner: QUOMODO

meat, a strong odor of burning: NIDOR

meek man who accepts his wife's adultery: WITTOL

meekness, mildness, or gentleness: MANSUETUDE

memory, by or from: MEMORITER

memory, false: PARAMNESIA

mental deficiency: AMENTIA, OLIGOPHRENIA

metal or plastic tube around each end of a shoelace: AGLET

metal plate around keyhole or doorknob: ESCUTCHEON

metaphorical: TRALATITIOUS

middle position, occupying: MESOTHETIC

mildness, meekness, or gentleness: MANSUETUDE

military retreat: KATABASIS

mind, smallness of: PARVANIMITY

minor dispute: VELITATION

miracle worker: THAUMATURGE

misrepresentation through suppressing or concealing facts:
    SUBREPTION

mixture or medley: FARRAGO

mob, government by: OCHLOCRACY

mock combat: SCIAMACHY

mocked, man who is: PILGARLIC

moderate or sparing in food or drink: ABSTEMIOUS

moderation or self-control: SOPHROSYNE

money, hoarding: PISMIRISM

moneymaking, motivated by: QUAESTUARY

monster-containing storytelling: TERATOLOGY

moocher: SCHNORRER

morally questionable: LOUCHE

morning love song: AUBADE

morning, occurring in or relating to the: MATUTINAL

morning-song: AUBADE

motivation, loss or lack of: ABULIA

move a child up and down on one's knees: DANDLE

moving about rapidly: VOLITANT

moving water, relating to or living in: LOTIC

mud-dwelling: LIMICOLOUS

murder of a wife by her husband: UXORICIDE

music created to greet the morning: AUBADE

nail biting: ONYCHOPHAGY

nasality in voice: RHINOPHONIA

naval supremacy: THALASSOCRACY

neighboring: LIMITROPHE

nervous irritability: FANTODS

nest, build a: NIDIFICATE

new, being hostile to what is: MISONEISTIC

newborn child, the first cry of a: VAGITUS

newsmonger: QUIDNUNC

night-blindness: NYCTALOPIA

night-wandering: NOCTIVAGANT

noise, great: TINTAMARRE

noisy: STREPITOUS

noisy quarrel: RUCTION

nonconformist: RECUSANT

nonsense that appears meaningful: AMPHIGORY

nose, fleshy bulbs on each side of the: ALAE

nose, having a long and narrow: LEPTORRHINIAN

O

obedient, one who is unquestioningly: MYRMIDON

obscene (especially in lyrics or verse): FESCENNINE

obscene or filthy literature, study of: COPROLOGY

obscenity, the worship of: AISCHROLATREIA

obsessed with words, person: LOGOMANIAC

odd and fanciful contrivance: WHIGMALEERIE

odor, having a strongly offensive: GRAVEOLENT

odor, offensive: FETOR

office, a craving for holding public: EMPLEOMANIA

offspring, love of: PHILOPROGENEITY

old and usually cantankerous woman: GRIMALKIN

old female cat: GRIMALKIN

old woman: GAMMER

one word, consisting of only: MONEPIC

open to the sky: HYPAETHRAL

opinion, false: PSEUDODOX

opponent of innovative technology: LUDDITE

optimist: AGATHIST

optimistic, blindly or naively: PANGLOSSIAN

organized badly: INCONDITE

other-regarding: ALTEROCENTRIC

out-and-out: ARRANT

outbreeding: EXOGAMY

outburst: FANTODS

outstanding: PALMARY

overbearing and quarrelsome woman: TERMAGANT

overcome by violence: SPIFLICATE

painful or difficult defecation: DYSCHEZIA

pain in the back: DORSODYNIA

pain in the butt: PYGALGIA

pamper: COSSET, DANDLE

parallel course, following a: PARADROMIC

passed along (as from one generation to another):
   TRALATITIOUS

past viewed as oppressively affecting the present:
   MORTMAIN

patience in adversity: LONGANIMITY

peace, promoting: IRENIC

peculiar to an individual: IDIOPATHIC

pedantic or academic expressions: SCHOLASMS

peddler of books (especially the Bible): COLPORTEUR

pedestrians, robber of: FOOTPAD

performer of miracles: THAUMATURGE

perspiration, smelly: KAKIDROSIS

pettiness: PARVANIMITY

philosopher, superficial: PHILOSOPHASTER

philosophy of life: WELTANSCHAUUNG

phony: BRUMMAGEM

pill, small: PARVULE

pit, bottomless: BARATHRUM

pit into which Athenian criminals were thrown:
  BARATHRUM

plant having flowers arising from the rootstock:
  AMPHIGEAN

plastic or metal tube around each end of a shoelace: AGLET

pleasure, inability to experience: ANHEDONIA

pleasure-seeker: FRANION

plump, pleasingly: ZAFTIG

plundering of food, as when members of one species steal
  food from another: CLEPTOBIOSIS

poison: VENENATE

political and social supremacy by males: ANDROCRACY

pompous or bombastic language: GRANDILOQUENCE

pound sign (#): OCTOTHORPE

poverty: ILLTH

practical, functional, or utilitarian: BANAUSIC

praiseworthy: PALMARY

preacher who stumbles through sermons: MARTEXT

pregnant: GRAVID

present, oppressive influence of the past on the:
  MORTMAIN

pretentious linguistic expression: LEXIPHANICISM

prize, award a: PREMIATE

procession, one who clears the way for a: WHIFFLER

proctor an examination: INVIGILATE

producing only females: THELYTOKOUS

production of many children: PHILOPROGENEITY

productive: FERACIOUS

profit-oriented or profit-seeking: QUAESTUARY

prolific or fruitful: FERACIOUS

promoting peace: IRENIC

prophetic: FATIDIC, MANTIC

prostitute: QUEAN

prostitution, house of: BAGNIO, LUPANAR

prostrate oneself on the ground: HUMICUBATE

prudish: PUDIBUND

psychoanalysis, one receiving: ANALYSAND

public office, mania for holding: EMPLEOMANIA

published falsehood: ROORBACK

pulling an all-nighter: PERNOCTATION

punch bowl with scalloped rim: MONTEITH

puritanical censor: WOWSER

purplish black: MURREY

questioning constantly: PYSMATIC

ragged clothing, person wearing: TATTERDEMALION

raging: FURIBUND

rapid and jerky eye movement (as during reading):
SACCADE

rapping sound: RATAPLAN

rascal: VARLET

reader, voracious: BIBLIOPHAGE

reading or having read everything: OMNILEGENT

real: VERIDICAL

reclining on a couch: ACCUBATION

red the color of bricks: LATERITIOUS

red the color of wine: VINACEOUS

redundancy: NIMIETY

redundant expression: PLEONASM

refined, affectedly: NIMINY-PIMINY

reincarnation: METEMPSYCHOSIS

religious skeptic or disbeliever: NULLIFIDIAN

remark, stupid: BÊTISE

remedy, universal: CATHOLICON

remodel a building without proper knowledge:
    GRIMTHORPE

repeat a word or sentence unconsciously and meaninglessly:
    VERBIGERATE

repetitive beating or rapping sound: RATAPLAN

repulsive odor, having a: GRAVEOLENT

restoration after decay, lapse, or dilapidation:
    INSTAURATION

restorative: ROBORANT

restore to an original state or condition: REPRISTINATE

retreat, military: KATABASIS

reverberating thunderously: TONITRUOUS

reverberation, loud: REBOATION

rich, preoccupied with becoming: C H R E M A T I S T I C

ringing of bells, pertaining to: T I N T I N N A B U L A R

riotous disturbance: R U C T I O N

rip to pieces: D I L A C E R A T E

risk or danger, expose to: P E R I C L I T A T E

robber of pedestrians: F O O T P A D

rock, composed of or inscribed on: R U P E S T R I A N

rodent, resembling a: G L I R I F O R M

rosy complexion: R U B I C U N D

rubbing one's body against others for sexual gratification:
  F R O T T A G E

rubbish, growing in: R U D E R A L

ruddy: R U B I C U N D

rumble, gurgle, or growl made by a distressed stomach:
  W A M B L E

rumbling sound of intestinal gas: B O R B O R Y G M U S

rural: V I L L A T I C

S

sad memories, drug or potion said to remove: N E P E N T H E

saints, worship of: H A G I O L A T R Y

savor: DEGUST

saying, terse: APOTHEGM

scanty: EXIGUOUS

scholarly writer: LUCUBRATOR

scholars collectively: CLERISY

scholastic or theological debate over a subtle point:
QUODLIBET

school: PHRONTISTERY

seclusion, carried on in: UMBRATILE

secretary, private (especially of a medieval scholar or
magician): FAMULUS

seizures about words, one given to: LOGOLEPT

self-control or moderation: SOPHROSYNE

self-sufficiency, economic: AUTARKY

selling, act of: VENDITION

semiconscious state between sleep and wakefulness,
pertaining to the: HYPNOPOMPIC

sentences of one word, consisting of: MONEPIC

set or place together: COLLOCATE

sewage: SULLAGE

sexual desire, uncontrollable and insatiable: LIBIDOCORIA

sexual gratification from rubbing one's body against others:
FROTTAGE

sexual intercourse in a parked car: AMOMAXIA

sexual intercourse without orgasm: ACRITITION

sexual pleasure from being whipped: MASTILAGNIA

shadow fighting: SCIAMACHY

shadows, dispersing: SCIALYTIC

shaking of the buttocks when walking: QUATOPYGIA

sham: BRUMMAGEM

sheeplike: OVINE

shoelace, plastic or metal tube around the end of: AGLET

short-winded: PURSY

shrew: TERMAGANT, XANTHIPPE

shyster: PETTIFOGGER

sickly person morbidly concerned about health:
    VALETUDINARIAN

sideburns, long flowing: DUNDREARIES

side by side: PARADROMIC

side scene: COULISSE

signature, a flourish made at the end of a: PARAPH

signature made by one person for another: ALLOGRAPH

sign or portent: OSTENT

silent, becoming or keeping: OBMUTESCENT

silly: ANSERINE

simple, rustic life, one leading a: ARCADIAN

sinning, capable of: PECCABLE

sinuous: FLEXUOUS

skeptic or disbeliever about religion: NULLIFIDIAN

skillful: HABILE

skirmish: VELITATION

sky, wholly or partly open to the: HYPAETHRAL

sleep, dispelling: HYPNOPOMPIC

sleep, one who talks in one's: SOMNILOQUIST

slender body, one having a: LEPTOSOME

slender toes, having: LEPTODACTYLOUS

slip of memory or tongue: PARAPRAXIS

sloppy and crude person: GROBIAN

sluggish: COSTIVE

sluglike: LIMACINE

slut: DRATCHELL, FRANION

smallness of mind: PARVANIMITY

small pill: PARVULE

small talk, pertaining to: PHATIC

smell of burning meat: NIDOR

smelly perspiration: KAKIDROSIS

smiling: SUBRISIVE

social and political supremacy by males: ANDROCRACY

soften: INTENERATE

soreness of the eyes: LIPPITUDE

sour juice: VERJUICE

sourness (as of disposition): VERJUICE

space between teeth: DIASTEMA

sparing or moderate in eating and drinking: ABSTEMIOUS

specialist in law: LEGIST

spiritual apathy and laziness: ACEDIA

spraying saliva while talking: SIALOQUENT

sprinkle: ASPERGE

spruce up: TITIVATE

stammering: TRAULISM

starchy: AMYLACEOUS

star-shaped: STELLIFORM

staying up all night (as when partying or studying):
    PERNOCTATION

still waters, relating to: LENTIC

stocky physique, having a: PYKNIC

stomach-growling: BORBORYGMUS

stone to death: LAPIDATE

storklike: PELARGIC

straight hair, having: LEIOTRICHOUS

stretching and yawning: PANDICULATION

strict adherence to one's chosen faith: ORTHOPRAXY

study or thought, a place for: PHRONTISTERY

stuffed (especially with finely ground meat): FARCI

stupid: DUNCICAL

stupid and culturally backward: BOEOTIAN

stuttering: TRAULISM

subtle or debatable point: QUODLIBET

sudden occurrence, pertaining to a: SUBITANEOUS

summer, of, relating to, or appearing in the: ESTIVAL

sun-worshiper: HELIOLATER

superciliousness: HAUTEUR

superficial philosopher: PHILOSOPHASTER

supervise an examination: INVIGILATE

surname: COGNOMEN

surrounding: CIRCUMJACENT

suspended by a thread: FILIPENDULOUS

swimming: NATATION

sword-shaped: XIPHOID

sycophant: LICKSPITTLE

symbol of the pound sign (#): OCTOTHORPE

take for one's own: SPHETERIZE

talkativeness, pathologically excessive and often incoherent: LOGORRHEA

talk excessively: POLYLOGIZE

talking with one's hands: HYPERMIMIA

talk noisily or captiously: BRABBLE

talks in one's sleep, one who: SOMNILOQUIST

taste with relish or delight: DEGUST

tear apart: DILACERATE

tearful: FLEBILE

technology, opponent of: LUDDITE

teeth, act of grinding of: BRUXOMANIA

teeth, gap between: DIASTEMA, EMBRASURE

temperance: SOPHROSYNE

temptation, susceptible to: PECCABLE

tentative: PEIRASTIC

testicles, without: ANORCHOUS

thinking, place for: PHRONTISTERY

third person, in reference to oneself: ILLEISM

thread, suspended by a: FILIPENDULOUS

thundering: TONITRUOUS

tic, person affected with a: TIQUEUR

tightrope walker: FUNAMBULIST

tiny creature: MINIMUS

toady: LICKSPITTLE

tobacco juice: AMBEER

toe, little: MINIMUS

toenail, crescent pale area at the base of: LUNULA

toes, having slender: LEPTODACTYLOUS

told orally to disciples only: ACROAMATIC

tongue: LINGUA

toothache: ODONTALGIA

transparent: LUCULENT, TRANSPICUOUS

traveler: VIATOR

traveling supplies: VIATICUM

trickery, done or obtained by: OBREPTITIOUS

truthful: VERIDICAL

turn or roll: WAMBLE

U

unclean: IMMUND

uncontrollable and insatiable sexual desire:
LIBIDOCORIA

uncontrollable urge to buy things: ONIOMANIA

understood clearly: LUCULENT, TRANSPICUOUS

unhappiness that is inescapable: ANHEDONIA

unhappy marriage: CAGAMOSIS

unknown cause, arising from: IDIOPATHIC

unmarried person: AGAMIST

unmelodious: SCRANNEL

unpolished (as in language): INCONDITE

unpredictable or random: ALEATORY

unprincipled person: VARLET

unprofitable or vain: FRUSTRANEOUS

unquestioningly and possibly ruthlessly obedient,
one who is: MYRMIDON

unwillingness: NOLITION

upper lip, vertical groove on: PHILTRUM

upset stomach: WAMBLE

urging strongly: HORTATORY

useful knowledge, devoted to: CHRESTOMATHIC

useless or ineffectual: FRUSTRANEOUS

utilitarian, practical, or functional: BANAUSIC

vacation: FERIATION

vain or unprofitable: FRUSTRANEOUS

veiling, act of: OBVELATION

vertical groove on upper lip: PHILTRUM

violin-shaped: PANDURIFORM

virgin, act of deflowering a: HYMENORRHEXIS

vital or living: ZOETIC

vivacity: BRIO

voice, extreme nasality in: RHINOPHONIA

wandering (and especially Scottish) beggar:
   GABERLUNZIE

wandering at night: NOCTIVAGANT

wart: VERRUCA

wasplike: VESPINE

waters that are moving (streams, rivers), relating to
or living in: LOTIC

waters that are still (ponds, lakes, swamps), relating to or
living in: LENTIC

waving hands while talking: HYPERMIMIA

wealth, pertaining to the pursuit of: CHREMATISTIC

wealth, worship of: PLUTOLATRY

weaning: ABLACTATION

whim: WHIGMALEERIE

whipped, sexual pleasure from being: MASTILAGNIA

whiskers of a cat: VIBRISSAE

whisper: SIFFILATE

white, growing: CANESCENT

widowhood: VIDUITY

wife, murder of one's: UXORICIDE

wild and unruly young person: RANTIPOLE

will, loss or lack of: ABULIA

winding or bending: FLEXUOUS

windows, having: FENESTRATED

wine, connoisseur of: OENOPHILIST

wine, having the color of red: VINACEOUS

wine lover: OENOPHILIST

winemaking, science of: ENOLOGY

wine, pertaining to: VINACEOUS

wintry: HIEMAL

wisdom, relating to: PALLADIAN

wish with no desire to expend energy to fulfill it: VELLEITY

without testicles: ANORCHOUS

woman, loose: DRATCHELL, FRANION

woman, nagging: TERMAGANT, XANTHIPPE

woman, old: GAMMER

woman, old and usually cantankerous: GRIMALKIN

woman without children: NULLIPARA

women, government by: GYNARCHY

wooded: BOSKY

wooden: TREEN

woodlike: XYLOID

words, person obsessed with: LOGOMANIAC

words, person who has seizures about: LOGOLEPT

working farm horse: DOBBIN

work, taking time off: FERIATION

world, relating to most of the: MONDIAL

worldview: WELTANSCHAUUNG

wormlike: VERMIFORM

worshiper of the sun: HELIOLATER

worship of foreign or unsanctioned gods: ALLOTHEISM

worship of obscenity or filth: AISCHROLATREIA

worship of saints: HAGIOLATRY

worship of wealth: PLUTOLATRY

worst people, government by the: KAKISTOCRACY

wrestling, pertaining to: PALAESTRAL

wrinkles, having many: RUGOSE

writer's cramp: GRAPHOSPASM

writing table or desk: ESCRITOIRE

yawning and stretching: PANDICULATION

yellow: XANTHIC

yesterday evening: YESTREEN

yesterday, relating to: PRIDIAN

yolk of an egg: VITELLUS

THE
APPENDIX

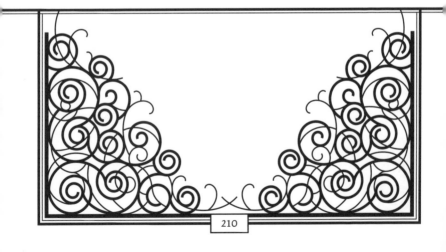

WEB SITES FOR WORD LOVERS

The following list contains Internet sites of dictionaries, glossaries, or search engines that will entertain and educate even the most learned word lover.

AllDictionaries.com (www.alldictionaries.com) A categorized index of language and subject dictionaries.

AlphaDictionary.com (www.alphadictionary.com/index.shtml) A search engine for 992 online dictionaries.

AskOxford.com (www.askoxford.com) A dictionary and a thesaurus.

A-Z-Dictionaries.com (http://a-z-dictionaries.com) A set of links to free online dictionaries.

Cambridge Dictionaries Online (http://dictionary.cambridge.org) An online dictionary from Cambridge University Press.

The Clear English Online Dictionary List (http://www.clearenglish.net/dictionary.htm) A large directory of online dictionaries, both English and bilingual, including specialist dictionaries.

CoolDictionary.com (www.cooldictionary.com) A free edition of a complete Webster dictionary, fully crosslinked, with audible pronunciations.

Dictionary.com (http://dictionary.reference.com) An online dictionary.

Directory.net (http://directory.net/Reference/Dictionaries) A directory with links to several dictionaries.

Glossarist (www.glossarist.com) A searchable directory of glossaries and topical dictionaries on many subjects.

Grandiloquent Dictionary (www.islandnet.com/~egbird/dict/dict.htm) A dictionary of rare and obscure words.

Infoplease (www.infoplease.com/dictionary.html) A dictionary search giving access to more than 125,000 entries.

Merriam-Webster OnLine (www.m-w.com) An online dictionary.

OneLook Dictionary Search (www.onelook.com) A search engine for looking up words in many dictionaries simultaneously.

The Phrontistery (http://phrontistery.info) A site for lovers of obscure, unusual, and interesting words; also contains glossaries of different topics (theology, units of measurement, numerical prefixes, and so on).

Spizzerinctum (www.spizzquiz.net/index.html) "Words You've Never Heard, and Events You'll Never Forget, in a Quiz!!"

Word Assault (www.wordassault.com) A site for looking up words in several databases.

Word Central (www.wordcentral.com) A student dictionary and rhyming dictionary of the Merriam-Webster Web site.

Wordsmyth (http://wordsmyth.net) A site of many unusual words.

Worthless Word For the Day (http://home.mn.rr.com/wwftd) A site specializing in extremely unusual words, but largely nontechnical ones, generally avoiding legal, medical, and other jargon.

SELECTED BIBLIOGRAPHY

The American Heritage Dictionary of the English Language, 3d ed. Boston: Houghton Mifflin, 1992.

Berent, Irwin M., and Rod L. Evans. *More Weird Words*. New York: Berkley Books, 1995.

Berent, Irwin M. *Weird Words*. New York: Berkley Books, 1995.

Bowler, Peter. *The Superior Person's Book of Words*. New York: Dell Laurel, 1982.

Bowler, Peter. *The Superior Person's Second Book of Weird and Wondrous Words*. Boston: D.R. Godine, 1992.

Brown, Roland Wilbur. *Composition of Scientific Words: A Manual of Methods and a Lexicon of Materials for the Practice of Logotechnics*. Washington, DC: Smithsonian Institution Press, 1956.

Dickson, Paul. *Dickson's Word Treasury: A Connoisseur's Collection of Old and New, Weird and Wonderful, Useful and Outlandish Words*. New York: John Wiley & Sons, 1992.

Elster, Charles Harrington. *There's A Word for It!: A Grandiloquent Guide to Life*. New York: Scribner, 1996.

Evans, Rod L. Sexicon: *The Ultimate X-Rated Dictionary*. New York: Citadel Press, 2002.

Evans, Rod L., and Irwin M. Berent. *Getting Your Words' Worth: Discovering and Enjoying Phantonyms, Gramograms, Anagrams, and Other Fascinating Word Phenomena*. New York: Warner Books, 1993.

Gause, John T. *The Complete University Word Hunter*. New York: Thomas Y. Crowell Co., 1967.

Grambs, David. *The Endangered English Dictionary: Bodacious Words Your Dictionary Forgot*. New York: W.W. Norton & Co., 1994.

Handford, S.A., and Mary Herberg. *Langenscheidt's Shorter Latin Dictionary*. Berlin, 1966.

Heifetz, Josefa (Mrs. Byrne). *Mrs. Byrne's Dictionary of Unusual, Obscure, and Preposterous Words*, new and exp. ed. Secaucus, NJ: Carol Publishing Group, 1994.

Hellweg, Paul. *The Insomniac's Dictionary: The Last Word on the Odd Word*. New York: Facts on File, 1986.

Hill, Robert, ed. *A Dictionary of Difficult Words*, rev. ed. New York: Gramercy Publishing Co., 1990.

Hook, J.N. *The Grand Panjandrum and 2,699 Other Rare, Useful, and Delightful Words and Expressions*, rev. ed. New York: Macmillan, 1991.

Lederer, Richard. *Adventures of a Verbivore*. New York: Pocket Books, 1994.

Lederer, Richard. Crazy English: *The Ultimate Joy Ride Through our Language*. New York: Pocket Books, 1989.

Lederer, Richard. *The Play of Words: Fun & Games for Language Lovers*. New York: Pocket Books, 1990.

Lewis, Norman. *The Comprehensive Word Guide*. Garden City, N.Y.: Doubleday, 1958.

McCutcheon, Marc. *Descriptionary: A Thematic Dictionary*. New York: Facts on File, 1992.

McKean, Erin, ed. *Weird and Wonderful Words*. New York: Oxford University Press, 2002.

Novobatzky, Peter, and Ammon Shea. *Depraved English*. New York: St. Martin's Press, 1999.

Partridge, Eric. *Origins: A Short Etymological Dictionary of Modern English*. New York: Greenwich House, 1983.

Rocke, Russell. *The Grandiloquent Dictionary*. Englewood Cliffs, N.J.: Prentice-Hall, 1972.

Saussy, George Stone III. *The Oxter English Dictionary: Uncommon Words Used by Uncommonly Good Writers*. New York: Facts on File, 1984.

Schmidt, J.E. *Lecher's Lexicon: An A-Z Encyclopedia of Erotic Expressions and Naughty Bits*. New York: Bell Publishing Co., 1984.

Schur, Norman W. *1000 Most Obscure Words*. New York: Facts on File, 1990.

Urdang, Laurence, ed. *Modifiers*. Detroit: Gale Research Co., 1982.

Urdang, Laurence. *The New York Times Everyday Reader's Dictionary of Misunderstood, Misused, and Mispronounced Words*. New York: Quadrangle/The New York Times Book Co., 1972.

Webster's Third New International Dictionary of the English Language, Unabridged. Springfield, Mass.: G. & C. Merriam Co., 1971.

Westley, Miles. *The Bibliophile's Dictionary*. Cincinnati, Ohio: Writer's Digest Books, 2005.